Islam

A SHORT HISTORY

'Few available guides to understanding Islam rival the concise cohesiveness and reliability of this addition to Watt's prolific output'
Publishers Weekly

'Will make an excellent text book for first year university students of religions'
JAMES THROWER in the *Expository Times*

'A reliable and perceptive guide by a master of the subject'
MARTIN FORWARD in the *Epworth Review*

'The author writes with clarity and sympathy'
ROBERT GLEAVE in the *Journal of Semitic Studies*

'Watt's is no mere pious history of Islam; it is also politically correct.'
ROBERT CARVER in *The Scotsman*

'For the adult reader coming fresh to the faith ... present[s] a clear and knowledgeable view'
MARK CRASTER-CHAMBERS in *Education Review*

OTHER BOOKS IN THIS SERIES:

OTHER BOOKS ON ISLAMIC STUDIES PUBLISHED BY ONEWORLD:

Islam

A SHORT HISTORY

William Montgomery Watt

ONEWORLD
OXFORD

ISLAM: A SHORT HISTORY

Oneworld Publications
(Sales and Editorial)
185 Banbury Road
Oxford OX2 7AR
England
http://www.oneworld-publications.com

Oneworld Publications
(US Marketing Office)
160 N. Washington Street
4th Floor, Boston
MA 02114
USA

ISBN 1–85168–205–8

Cover design by Design Deluxe
Typeset by LaserScript, Mitcham
Printed and bound in England by Clays Ltd, St Ives plc

CONTENTS

INTRODUCTION

The primary purpose of this book is to provide the Western reader with a positive understanding of Islam, of its origin, its history and its beliefs; but it is hoped that there may also be something of value in it for the Muslim reader. It is based on the belief that Muhammad was a prophet chosen by God for a particular task, and also that God was behind the spread of Islam throughout the world. At the same time, this book accepts the main principles of the Western intellectual outlook, including its historical criticism; and consequently departs from some of the traditional ideas of Muslims about the history of their religion.

In the presentation of Islamic beliefs the Qur'an is widely used, and the translation is my own. I have deviated at two small points from the standard transliteration of Arabic words and names. First, while the Arabic definite article 'al' is always written with 'l', in certain cases it is assimilated in speech to the following consonant, and here I have indicated the pronunciation. Second, in proper names where a dependent genitive is virtually inseparable from the previous word, I have indicated this by a hyphen. Thus Ibn-Zayd means 'the son of Zayd' and 'Abd-Allah means 'the slave (or servant) of God'. (The New Testament frequently uses the word 'slave' (*doulos*), but this became *servus* in Latin and then 'servant' in English.)

1 THE BEGINNINGS

1. ARABIA AND MECCA BEFORE ISLAM

For an understanding of the early history of the religion of Islam, it is necessary to know something of the conditions of life in Arabia at that time. Most of the inhabitants of Arabia belonged to nomadic tribes, although there were also some settled tribes or parts of tribes and some small towns, such as Mecca. The nomads gained a livelihood by pasturing camels and other animals and this way of life was dictated by geographical conditions. In much of the country rainfall was scanty and erratic. After the main period of rain some areas would have lush vegetation for a few weeks and a tribe would move there, but when the vegetation was exhausted they would have to resort to areas where there were wells and perennial shrub. Each tribe thus required a much greater area than it occupied at any one time. There was some understanding about the area in which a tribe had a right to pasture, and a strong tribe would maintain this right by force. When a tribe became too weak to maintain its rights, it could appeal to a strong tribe for support and protection, and such relationships were common.

The nomadic Arabs are said to have had many gods, but these do not seem to have meant much to them. They firmly believed that the main events in a person's life were determined by an impersonal force called Time or Fate. As the Qur'an puts it, 'They say, There is nought but this present life; we die and we live, and only Time destroys us' (45.24). Their deepest belief seems to have been what might be called tribal humanism, and this was fostered by the strong tradition of poetry. The poets celebrated the exploits of individual heroes, but these were seen as being due to the high qualities present in the tribal stock rather than to anything personal; and most of the Arabs felt that this was what made life meaningful. There was also what might be called a code of ethics associated with the tribal system. In this, a tribe or clan as a whole was held responsible for the misdemeanours of its members, and the principle of a life for a life was generally observed. This often led to serious and long-lasting blood feuds, and these were one of the problems facing Muhammad. There was also an expectation that the leading men of a tribe would show some concern for the tribe's weaker members.

Mecca had a somewhat exceptional position. It was not an oasis, but there was sufficient well water to support a small settled community. This had grown up round a sacred shrine, the Ka'ba, which was roughly cubical in shape and had 'the black stone' built into one corner. This may have been a meteorite and was regarded as having divine properties. The area round the Ka'ba, known as the Haram, was specially sacred, and a wider area round Mecca had a degree of sacredness. This made it possible to have annual fairs not far from Mecca to which the nomads could come, since within the sacred area tribal feuds were in abeyance. Among the tribes too certain months were regarded as sacred and it was during these months that the fairs were held. In consequence of this, Mecca was an important commercial centre.

In the sixth century CE Greater Syria and Egypt were part of the Byzantine empire, while Iraq was part of the Sassanian (Persian) empire. Incessant wars between the two empires had disrupted the trade route by way of Iraq from India and the Persian Gulf to the Mediterranean at Aleppo. The merchants of Mecca had taken advantage of this situation and by about CE 600 most of that trade was carried by their camel caravans from the Yemen via Mecca to Gaza, Damascus and Aleppo. They also controlled various enterprises along the route, and had been unscrupulous in excluding non-Meccans, such as Yemenis, from the caravan trade. As a result they had acquired considerable wealth; but in the process their ethical standards had slipped. The traditional ethics of Mecca had been that of the nomadic tribes, but this was not altogether appropriate for a commercial community. They could also prefer business associates from other clans to members of their own, and they often neglected the traditional duties of clan chiefs (which most of them were) to look after the poorer and weaker members of their own clans.

Nearly all the inhabitants of Mecca belonged to the tribe of Quraysh, but there were also craftsmen from the Byzantine empire and elsewhere who spent long periods in Mecca. Quraysh were divided into about a dozen clans, which sometimes formed two or three rival groups. Common commercial interests, however, prevented any serious clashes between clans or groups of clans.

2. MUHAMMAD'S EARLY LIFE AND CALL

Muhammad belonged to the clan of Hashim, of which his grandfather 'Abd-al-Muttalib had been chief. Like other leading men in the clans, 'Abd-al-Muttalib had been a merchant, but possibly not so important and so commercially successful as the later biographers of Muhammad make out. Muhammad's father, 'Abd-Allah, had also been a merchant, but he had died in Medina on the way back from a trip to Syria while Muhammad's mother, Amina, was pregnant with him.

Muhammad's birth is thought to have taken place in or around the year CE 570. He was at first in the care of his mother, but she died when he was aged six. For a time he had been given to a wet-nurse belonging to a nomadic tribe, because life in the steppe was thought to be healthier for infants than that in Mecca, and many Meccan women did this. After Amina's death, Muhammad was looked after by his grandfather 'Abd-al-Muttalib, until his death when Muhammad was eight; and then an uncle, Abu-Talib, took charge of him. When he was old enough, Muhammad went on trading journeys to Syria with his uncle. As a result of the experience he had gained in this way, a wealthy widow named Khadija, herself a merchant, commissioned him to look after her goods on a journey to Syria. Well satisfied with his fulfilment of the commission, she offered him her hand in marriage and he accepted. He is said to have been twenty-five, while she was forty, but she is also said to have borne him six or more children, some boys who died and four girls, Umm-Kulthum, Zaynab, Ruqayya and Fatima. After the marriage, Muhammad was able to use his wife's capital to trade on their account along with a partner. Previously he had had no capital of his own because a person below a certain age was not allowed to inherit, and so nothing had come to him from his father or grandfather. Doubtless this custom originated among the nomads, since obviously a minor could not look after a herd of camels.

Muhammad was a thoughtful person and was in the habit of making a retreat each year in a cave on Mount Hira, close to Mecca. There he presumably meditated on religious matters and on the social problems which increasing wealth was creating in the Meccan community. Of these he was probably specially aware because of his own exclusion for a time from the main trading activities until he married Khadija. In a particular year, when he was about forty, he had a strange experience. He heard a voice saying to him, 'Recite.' He responded, 'What shall I recite?' and the voice went on, 'Recite, in the name of thy Lord who created – created man from a blood-clot. Recite, for thy Lord is bountiful, who taught by the Pen, taught man what he knew not.' This is the opening passage of Surat al-'Alaq (96) of the Qur'an. Muhammad was puzzled by this experience, but when he returned home and told Khadija about it, she talked to her kinsman Waraqa, who had some knowledge of the Bible and may have been a Christian, and Waraqa expressed the view that what had thus come to Muhammad was similar to what had come to Moses. Partly because of what Waraqa had said and perhaps partly for other reasons, Muhammad came to regard the words he had heard and then recited as a revelation from God.

This account of the receiving of the first revelation is probably the true one, but it should be noted that there is another version. The word here translated as 'recite' is *iqra*', but it can also mean 'read'. Muhammad's reply was *ma aqra'u*, and this can mean either 'What shall I recite/read?' or 'I do not recite/read.' The less likely version of the story takes the original voice to have meant 'read', and Muhammad's reply to mean 'I do not read.' It seems clear, however, that this second interpretation of the events is due to later scholars who held the view that Muhammad was illiterate, thus proving the divine origin of the messages he received. They also interpreted the Qur'anic words *an-nabi al-ummi* applied to Muhammad as 'the illiterate Prophet', although for the original hearers the word *ummi* probably meant 'gentile' or 'non-Jewish'.

Muhammad himself firmly insisted that he had not composed the Qur'an, but it had come to him from beyond himself; and sound scholarship requires that this claim be accepted. He also believed that the Qur'an ultimately came from God; and this also should be accepted by non-Muslims in the inter-faith conditions of the end of the twentieth century. The earliest Christian critics of the Qur'an, however, such as John of Damascus (d. 750), who did secretarial work for a Muslim governor, knew of the references in it to Biblical characters, and so thought that Muhammad himself had put it together using what he had learned from the Bible. It was to counter this assertion that the doctrine of Muhammad's illiteracy was elaborated by Muslim scholars. Actually it is not a good argument, because even if Muhammad could not read, he could have had the Bible read to him or the stories related to him; and presumably there were some people in Mecca, like Waraqa, who had a slight knowledge of the Bible. Careful examination of the Qur'an today, however, shows that its knowledge of Biblical stories and events is minimal, whereas it contains much deep truth about the being of God and his dealings with the human race. This is a strong reason why the non-Muslim should accept the belief that somehow or other the Qur'an comes from God.

There is another passage which is sometimes said to be the first revealed. It runs:

O immantled one,
Rise and warn;
Thy Lord magnify,
Thy raiment purify,
The Wrath flee,
Give not to gain more,
For thy Lord endure.

(74.1–7)

It seems probable that this was not the first of all revelations but that the words, 'Rise and warn' mark the point at which

Muhammad had to proclaim the divine message publicly, and thus was the beginning of his public ministry. Many commentators think that 'wrath' should be translated 'abomination' and in practice means idolatry. The word 'immantled' may mean that Muhammad had put on a mantle or cloak as a protection against the unseen powers, or else to induce a revelation.

Muhammad continued to receive revelations from God at intervals for the rest of his life with a short gap in the earlier years. These revelations were in the first place recited and memorized by Muhammad and the followers he came to have. Later they were collected, partly by Muhammad himself and partly also afterwards by others. Muhammad had some written down for him, and one or two followers wrote down revelations for themselves. These revelations constitute the Qur'an or 'recitation' as we have it. The revelations came in different ways at different times. Some of these ways are mentioned in a verse: 'It was not for a human being that God should speak to him except by revelation, or from behind a veil, or that he should send a messenger to reveal [to him] what [God] willed by his permission' (42.51).

The messenger mentioned here is the angel Gabriel, for in another verse the words are addressed to Muhammad: 'Say, Who is an enemy to Gabriel? It is he who brought down this [revelation] upon your heart confirming what was present' (2.97). (The last phrase refers to previous scriptures.) Muslim scholars made lists of 'the manners of revelation' and found several besides those mentioned in the verse, though their precise interpretation of details is sometimes different. They held that in Muhammad's later years the revelations were normally brought by Gabriel. The first revelation, however, as described above, seems to have been no more than the hearing of a voice.

3. THE RESPONSE AT MECCA

From the beginning Muhammad shared with his wife, Khadija, the messages that came to him by revelation, and she was the first person to accept him as prophet and so become a Muslim. He went on to communicate the messages to ever widening circles, beginning with his family. This included his cousin 'Ali, son of Abu-Talib, then a boy of nine or ten, whom Muhammad was looking after, and also Zayd ibn-Haritha, probably in his late twenties, who had been given to Khadija as a slave and, on being given his freedom, decided to remain with her and Muhammad. Another early Muslim was Muhammad's closest friend, Abu-Bakr, a man two years younger than he was. Muslim scholars argue about which of these three was the first male Muslim, but the matter is not important for the general understanding of Islam.

As time went on, the messages were communicated to more and more of Muhammad's friends and acquaintances, but in private, as it were. The beginning of his public preaching is usually placed in the year 613, three years after he received the first revelation. Round about the same time he is said to have made his daytime base in the house of al-Arqam, and to have had thirty-nine followers. Al-Arqam was a wealthy young man who had a house in central Mecca which he allowed Muhammad to use as a meeting place for those who were interested in his message. This arrangement lasted only a short time, and in later periods Muslims liked to boast that their ancestors had become Muslims before Muhammad entered the house of al-Arqam or while he was there.

The majority of those who joined Muhammad in the first few years were young men from the wealthiest and most powerful families and clans – younger brothers or sons or cousins of the leading merchants. There were also men from less powerful clans who were slightly older, though none seems to have been more than thirty-five, except Abu-Bakr. A few others were persons from beyond Mecca, such as nomadic tribesmen or Abyssinian slaves, whose nominal clan protection might not be effective. Arabs from outside Mecca became confederates of a clan, but this was not an inferior status and one Arab confederate was reckoned head of the Meccan clan.

It is important to understand what attracted these men to the new religion Muhammad was preaching. To do so, however, one has to look at the points emphasized in the earliest revelations. The Qur'an is not arranged in chronological order, but both Muslim and non-Muslim scholars have spent much effort in trying to date the various suras and passages at least approximately. Though there is still much disagreement about dating, in those passages which would be widely accepted as early there are five points which feature prominently.

1. There is much about God's goodness and power. The passage commonly regarded as the earliest (96.1–8) speaks of God's creating the human being from a blood-clot (or embryo), and this is elaborated in other passages. Then there are references to God's creative power in nature:

> Will they not consider the camels, how they are created,
> The heaven, how it is raised,
> The mountains, how they are fixed,
> The earth, how it is spread.
>
> (88.17–20)

God's goodness is shown by the way in which he provides food or sustenance for his creatures:

> We showered the water in showers,
> Then fissured the earth in fissures,
> And caused to grow in it grain,
> And grapes and clover,
> And olives and palms,
> And orchards dense,
> And fruits and pasturage.
>
> (80.25–31)

2. There will be a day in the future – the Last Day or the Day of Judgement – when human beings will be brought before God to be judged in respect of the upright or wicked character of their lives in this world. The good will go to Paradise (or heaven) and the evil to hell. The words 'Rise and warn' (74.2) are a reference to this judgement. The more frightening descriptions of hell in the Qur'an, however, do not occur in the earliest passages. A relatively full early account is:

> When the heaven shall be rent
> And obey its Lord and be right,
> When the earth shall be levelled
> And spew those in it and be void
> And obey its Lord and be right,
> O man, thou art toiling heavily to thy Lord
> and meeting him.
> Who gets his book in his right
> Shall be reckoned with easily
> And return to his folk rejoicing;
> Who gets his book behind his back
> Shall invoke destruction
> And feed a furnace.
>
> (84.1–12)

3. Because God is powerful and good, the response of human beings should be to worship him and be grateful to him. From the earliest days, Muslims seem to have joined Muhammad in the Muslim prayer or formal worship (*salat*), and this included kneeling and touching the ground with one's forehead in acknowledgement of the supreme power of God and one's own littleness before him.

4. God also expects people to be generous with their wealth. Muhammad himself was told, 'As for the orphan, oppress not. As for the beggar, refuse not' (93.9–10). What was presumably a common attitude to wealth among the Meccans was condemned:

> Woe to every slanderer, scoffer,
> Who gathers wealth and counts it,
> Thinking wealth will make him immortal.
>
> (104.1–3)

A description is given of a person who will be adversely treated on the Last Day:

> He was not believing in God Almighty
> Nor urging to feed the destitute;
> Today he has no friend here.
>
> (69.33–5)

Some of these verses are not among the very earliest, but they are all fairly early. The interesting point is that the generous use of wealth is virtually the only aspect of human conduct mentioned in verses of this date.

5. There is a little about Muhammad's personal vocation. He was to 'Rise and warn' (74.2), to be one who reminds (87.9). In

other words, his primary function was to convey the messages he had received to those for whom they were intended. It was only later, after opposition had developed, that he became the leader of those who accepted the messages and was called 'prophet' (*nabi*) and 'the messenger of God' (*rasul Allah*). The latter has become the normal way for Muslims to refer to him; *rasul* means 'one sent' and so is similar to 'apostle', but the translation 'messenger' is now usually preferred.

A consideration of these five points helps us to understand what attracted people to accept the revelations received by Muhammad. There had been a breakdown of the old tribal humanism, of the old pride in the achievements of one's tribe or clan. The wealthiest clan chiefs had become individualists, neglecting their traditional duties. Those not in the inner circles of wealth and power felt that life had become largely meaningless. The Qur'an was insisting that the ultimate meaning of life was not to be found in the accumulation of wealth and power, and that the wealthy merchants were not so wealthy as they thought they were, since over them was an all-powerful God. Life would be meaningful if one lived uprightly, as God expected human beings to do. It is not surprising that many people, especially young men, became enthusiastic Muslims.

Because the Qur'an attacked some of the attitudes of the wealthy merchants, opposition to the new religion soon appeared among them. One of the leaders of this was Abu-Jahl, of the clan of Makhzum, a man of about Muhammad's age. One outward expression of this opposition was that some of the wealthiest men made life difficult for junior members of their own clans who had joined Muhammad. Clan solidarity prevented action against members of other clans, but within a clan the leading men still had great power.

In this connection it is appropriate to say something about the story of the so-called 'satanic verses', since the matter has recently gained some notoriety. The story comes from Islamic sources, and there are slightly different versions, but the main points seem to be as follows. Muhammad was sitting in the Ka'ba (the sacred area in the centre of Mecca), along with some of the rich merchants, wishing that he might receive a revelation which would win them over. At this moment he began to receive a revelation which ran:

> Have you considered Allat and al-'Uzza
> And Manat, the third, the other?
> Those are the swans exalted;
> Their intercession is expected;
> Their likes are not neglected.

The three deities named had shrines in the neighbourhood of Mecca. The merchants took the verses as meaning that prayer at these shrines was permissible, and thereupon joined with Muhammad in his act of worship. Later (but how much later is not clear) Muhammad came to realize that there was something wrong with this revelation, and he eventually received another to replace it:

> Have you considered Allat and al-'Uzza
> And Manat, the third, the other?
> For you males and for him [God] females?
> That would be unfair sharing.
> They are but names you and your fathers named;
> God revealed no authority for them;
> they [the worshippers] follow only opinion and their
> souls' fancies,
> though from their Lord there has come to them guidance.

$$(15.19–23)$$

It is difficult to understand how Muhammad ever came to accept the first form of this passage. The most likely explanation would seem to be that he regarded the three as angelic beings wholly subordinate to God, and not as deities. The word translated 'swans' is obscure and could have some such interpretation. The second version, now a part of the Qur'an, is a clear rejection of polytheism, and is a standard part of Islamic teaching, though the point does not occur in the earliest revelations.

Because of the suggestion that Muhammad could be deceived by Satan, many contemporary Muslims regard the story of the satanic verses as an invention by opponents of Islam, but this is not borne out by the sources. There is actually a verse in the Qur'an which asserts that prophets have sometimes been deceived by Satan: 'Before you [Muhammad] God sent no messenger or prophet but, when he desired, Satan interposed [something] towards his desire; but God abrogates what Satan interposes; then God perfects his verses; God is knowing wise' (22.51). In the commentaries on this verse, the story is told by some of the most reliable of Qur'an commentators such as al-Baydawi. In view of the Qur'anic verse and of the commentaries, it would seem that there may be some truth in the story.

Another event which resulted from the opposition to Muhammad was the emigration of a considerable number of Muslims to Abyssinia, where they were well received by the Negus or emperor. Here again there are slight divergences between different accounts of the emigration, but the main facts seem clear. In all about seventy Muslims are said to have gone to Abyssinia in two groups, first one of ten people and then a larger one; but it seems more likely that there were a number of small groups and that the emigration was spread over several years, beginning about 615. Some of these emigrants returned to Mecca after a short period and then later joined in the emigration to Medina. Others remained in Abyssinia until 628, when Muhammad invited them to join him in Medina. It seems clear that one of the reasons for the emigration was to avoid persecution, since most of those who emigrated came from the clans in which the wealthy merchants were making life difficult for their fellow clansmen. Those Muslims who remained in Mecca belonged to clans where this was not happening.

It seems possible, however, that there were other reasons for the emigration. One such would be to engage in trade, since the Meccans were primarily traders, and those who remained in Abyssinia until 628 must have been gaining a living by trading. It is also possible that Muhammad may have encouraged the emigration for other reasons at which we can only guess.

From about 615 Abu-Jahl seems to have been directing the opposition to Muhammad. He tried to persuade Abu-Talib, as head of the clan of Hashim, to withdraw clan protection from Muhammad; but Abu-Talib refused to do this, although he did not believe in Muhammad's religion. It was perhaps about 616 that Abu-Jahl then arranged for most of the clans of Quraysh to boycott the clan of Hashim. The boycott, however, may have helped the wealthy merchants more than it harmed Hashim, and after a year or two it disintegrated. About 619 Abu-Talib died, and around the same time Muhammad also lost his wife, Khadija, who had been the greatest support to him. As long as she lived, he took no other wife.

Abu-Talib had also supported Muhammad by maintaining clan protection, but his brother Abu-Lahab, who succeeded him, had done well as a merchant and had business associations with some of the very wealthy men hostile to Muhammad. Under pressure from them, he seems to have decided to withdraw clan protection from Muhammad unless he stopped preaching and teaching. This is doubtless the reason for the bitter attack on

Abu-Lahab in Sura 111 of the Qur'an. Abu-Lahab is said to have justified his decision by asserting that Muhammad had dishonoured his grandfather 'Abd-al-Muttalib, a former chief of the clan, by stating that he was in hell.

One of the ways in which Muhammad tried to deal with the situation created by Abu-Lahab was to undertake a journey to at-Ta'if. This was a small town about forty miles east of Mecca, with a better climate because it was higher up. For a time it had been a trade rival of Mecca, but now some of the rich Meccans had acquired houses and estates there, and the town was mainly under their control. Muhammad may have hoped to get support from those local people who disliked the Meccan presence, but in this he was disappointed. Instead of giving him support, the people he approached encouraged the mob to throw stones at him. Dejectedly Muhammad returned homewards, but before he could enter Mecca he had to obtain clan protection. It was only the third clan chief he approached who was prepared to give this, and doubtless it was with the understanding that he would greatly reduce his religious activities.

Muhammad is also said to have approached four nomadic tribes while they were at fairs in the neighbourhood, but not much seems to have come of this. There was a real breakthrough, however, during the annual pilgrimage to Mecca in June 620. Six pilgrims from Medina met Muhammad and were so impressed by his personality and message that five of them came to him again at the pilgrimage of 621, bringing with them seven other men. As a result of this meeting, the twelve agreed to accept Muhammad as the prophet, to obey him and to avoid various sins; this was known as the First Pledge of al-'Aqaba. It was also understood that Muhammad would be made welcome in Medina, since the twelve represented most shades of opinion there.

To prepare the way for Muhammad and perhaps also to ensure that conditions there were generally favourable, Muhammad sent one of his most trusted followers to Medina with the twelve. This man gave instruction in Islam to the people of Medina, and his work was so successful that no less than seventy-five persons, including two women, came to Mecca for the pilgrimage in June 622. These met Muhammad secretly at night and took a pledge not merely to accept Muhammad as the prophet and to avoid sins but also to fight for God and his messenger. This is the Second Pledge of al-'Aqaba or the Pledge of War.

Most of the Muslims in Mecca now emigrated to Medina in small groups. By September 622 all who intended to leave Mecca had departed, apart from Muhammad, Abu-Bakr, 'Ali and some of their families. By this time the hostile Meccans had become suspicious and are said to have plotted to kill Muhammad. He and Abu-Bakr then had to make a secret escape by night, leaving 'Ali sleeping in Muhammad's bed. In due course they safely reached Medina, where there was a warm welcome for them. This move of Muhammad and the other Muslims to Medina is known as the Hijra or Emigration (formerly sometimes translated 'flight'). The Islamic system of dating begins with the first day of the Arab year in which the Hijra took place – 16 June 622 – but the Islamic year has only twelve lunar months and so may begin at any part of our solar year. Islamic dates may be indicated by the letters AH (Anno Hegirae). The Meccan Muslims in Medina are known as the Emigrants, while the original inhabitants who became Muslims are the Helpers (Ansar).

The acceptance of Islam by most of the inhabitants of Medina arose out of the situation there at the time. Medina was an oasis extending to some twenty square miles where it was possible to grow dates and cereals. It lies over 250 miles north of

Mecca. In 622 there were eight strong Arab clans which controlled the oasis, but there were also three Jewish clans which had formerly been stronger than the Arabs and still held some of the best lands. It is not clear whether these clans were of Hebrew descent or whether they were Arabs who had adopted Judaism. Culturally there was little difference between them and the Arabs. There were also some smaller groups of Arabs subservient to the Jews and perhaps also some smaller groups of Jews.

Unfortunately there had been much quarrelling among the Arab clans, and this had culminated in the battle of Bu'ath in 618. In this nearly all the Arab clans had been involved on one side or the other, and probably most of the Jewish clans, since each was allied to an Arab clan. After the battle, peace had not been completely restored; and almost certainly many of the Arabs of Medina became Muslims because they hoped that Muhammad would be able to mediate between the warring factions and restore complete peace. Muhammad was careful not to marry any woman of Medina and so ally himself with one party. The Arabs of Medina may also have been ready to accept Muhammad as a prophet because they had heard the Jews speak of the coming of a Messiah who would set all things right for them. In a sense the troubles of Medina arose from the breakdown of nomadic morality in a settled situation; but Medina, as an oasis practising agriculture, was in a different position from Mecca as a commercial centre, even though there was a little commerce at Medina.

4. MUHAMMAD'S YEARS AT MEDINA

A document has been preserved which is often called the Constitution of Medina (the text will be found in my *Muhammad at Medina*, pp. 221–5). In the form in which we have it, it contains nearly fifty articles, some of them somewhat repetitive. Scholars generally accept its authenticity but disagree about its dating and how it has been put together. It seems fairly certain that the main articles represent the agreement made between Muhammad and the Muslims of Medina before he actually emigrated there, but that other articles have been added at later dates. Basically the document creates a federation between the tribe or clan of Emigrants from Mecca and eight clans of Arabs of Medina. Such a federation remained the nominal form of the Islamic state until after the fall of the Umayyad dynasty in 750, though many other Arab clans and tribes were added to it in Muhammad's lifetime and later. Non-Arab Muslims had to become clients of one of the Arab clans in the federation. The Jews of Medina were also provided for in a subordinate position. The three main Jewish clans are not named, but there are articles about Jewish groups associated (in a kind of clientship) with the Arab clans. Muhammad is accepted as the prophet, and it is also stated that serious disputes in the community are to be referred to him.

A few days after his arrival in Medina, Muhammad found a suitable site near the centre of the oasis and set about having a house built for himself. This eventually had a large central courtyard, sometimes used for formal prayers, while on the east side there were separate apartments for the various wives he now began to acquire. The names are listed of a dozen women who became his wives or concubines, and there are further lists of those whose possible marriage to Muhammad had been discussed. Virtually all his marriages had what might be called a political motive. Before he left Mecca he had married the widow of an early Muslim, in part no doubt to prevent her being married to a pagan. After coming to Medina he married 'A'isha and Hafsa, daughters of his two chief supporters, the later caliphs,

Abu-Bakr and 'Umar. While 'A'isha was the only virgin Muhammad married, Hafsa was the widow of a Muslim killed at Badr. These marriages thus created a close link between Muhammad and the two fathers. There were similar reasons behind his other marriages, and also behind the marriages of his daughters. After the death of Muhammad and his wives, his house in Medina became the central mosque there.

In the period after the Hijra, the biographers of Muhammad say little about what was happening in Medina but much about the *maghazi* or expeditions, and some eighty of these are mentioned. They varied from small affairs in which less than half a dozen men took part, sometimes only one, to large expeditions, such as that of 10,000 men to which Mecca surrendered, and that of 30,000 men to Tabuk. In a sense these were an extension of the nomadic razzia or raid (a word derived from the Arabic root present in *maghazi*), but they had many different aims, such as winning over tribes to support the Muslims and punishing them for attacks on Muslim camels. Many of them were attacks on Meccan trade caravans, and because of this the history of the period becomes the history of the armed struggle between the Muslims and the Meccan pagans. Only a few of the expeditions were led by Muhammad himself.

In the course of the year 623 there were several attempts by the Emigrants in Medina to intercept Meccan caravans, but none was successful, probably because people in Medina not friendly to Muhammad were sending warnings to the Meccans. The first successful expedition was in January 624. A small group of men was sent eastwards with sealed orders not to be opened until the end of the second day. These orders told them to go south to Nakhla, on the road between at-Ta'if and Mecca. Here, pretending to be pilgrims, they joined a Meccan caravan coming from the Yemen. After a day or so, while still outside the

Meccan sacred area, they attacked the four men guarding the caravan, killed one and took two prisoners. They then managed to reach Medina safely with the caravan and their prisoners. Some people were worried because the attack had taken place during a sacred month, but a verse of the Qur'an was revealed justifying the action (2.217). In the course of time there were other verses encouraging the Muslims to take part in fighting against the Meccans.

In March 624 Muhammad himself led an expedition of some three hundred men to the coast road used by caravans from Mecca to Syria; he was hoping to intercept a rich caravan returning from Gaza. Over two hundred of Muhammad's force were Helpers, and this was the first time these had joined an expedition in such numbers. The caravan, led by Abu-Sufyan of the clan of Umayya with seventy men, managed by forced marches and taking devious routes to elude the Muslims. Mecca, however, had received advance warning of Muhammad's plan, and Abu-Jahl collected a force of nearly a thousand men to go to protect the caravan. Though he was informed of the caravan's safety, he did not at once turn back to Mecca, but some of his men may have done so. Perhaps he wanted to teach Muhammad a lesson. A battle followed in which the Meccans were severely defeated, with between forty and seventy killed and seventy taken prisoner. Abu-Jahl himself was among those killed.

The defeat was a severe blow for the Meccans, since apart from the actual casualties it meant a loss of prestige, and that would in due course adversely affect their trading operations. Abu-Sufyan at once took charge of affairs in Mecca, and made preparations to inflict a defeat on the Muslims and restore Meccan prestige. By March 625 he had managed to collect a force of 3,000 men, including a cavalry force of 200. With these he marched on Medina, entered the oasis from its north-west

corner and camped in fields of grain there. In the centre of the
oasis there were numerous strongholds in which people were
secure from armed attack. Nevertheless, Muhammad decided to
confront the Meccans and managed to get 700 men to the hill of
Uhud, to the north of the Meccans. When the Meccans attacked,
the Muslims repulsed them and were moving towards the
Meccan camp, when they in turn were attacked in the rear by
the Meccan cavalry. In the following confusion, Muhammad and
most of his men regained the hill of Uhud, where they were safe
from the Meccan cavalry. However, other Muslims made for
their strongholds, and many of these were cut down. Altogether
the Muslims lost over seventy men, as against some twenty-seven
Meccans. The Meccans did not attempt any further attacks on
the Muslims, however, but after a short delay turned back to
Mecca. Although the Meccans had the better of the battle in
terms of casualties, they had completely failed in their primary
aim, which was to get rid of the threat to their commerce posed
by Muhammad and the Muslims in Medina.

The Meccans did not let the matter rest, but the next
outstanding event was the siege of Medina in April 627. For
this they had a force said to amount to 10,000 men, including
various nomadic tribes whom they had induced to join them.
This siege of Medina is known in the sources as the expedition of
the Khandaq or Trench. In order to protect the central part of the
oasis, where most of the dwellings were, Muhammad had caused
a trench to be dug. This central portion was protected by lava
flows on the east, south and west, and was open only on the
north. For a fortnight the Meccans tried in vain to cross the
trench, but by that time, because of the lack of results, they were
having difficulty in holding their motley force together and they
decided to retire. This withdrawal marked the utter failure of the
Meccans to remove Muhammad. After the fiasco of the siege, his

position was much stronger both in Medina itself and in the eyes of many of the nomadic tribes.

From this point onwards, Muhammad was not thinking so much of defeating the Meccans as of winning them over. Already in 624 the qibla (direction to be faced in prayer) had been changed from Jerusalem to Mecca. Now he seems to have wanted to show that the pilgrimage to Mecca would still have a place in his religion. In March 628 he went towards Mecca with almost 1,500 men, claiming that he wanted to make the 'Umra or Lesser Pilgrimage. The Meccans barred his way, but eventually in the treaty of al-Hudaybiya agreed to allow him to make the 'Umra in the following year. There were also other provisions aimed at improving relations between the Meccans and the Muslims. In March 629 Muhammad and about 2,000 Muslims actually made the 'Umra.

Towards the end of 629 there was an incident involving a tribe allied to Muhammad and one allied to the Meccans. This was formally a breach of the treaty and Muhammad decided to bring things to a head. Several leading Meccans had already become Muslims, and Muhammad knew that Abu-Sufyan was ready to compromise; in 628 Muhammad had married Abu-Sufyan's daughter Umm-Habiba after her Muslim husband had died. He therefore marched on Mecca with 10,000 men. Abu-Sufyan and other leaders came out to Muhammad and surrendered, being given an assurance that there would be a general amnesty. Muhammad's forces then occupied Mecca with negligible opposition. Muhammad remained in Mecca for two or three weeks, cleansed the Ka'ba of idols and made arrangements for the future administration of the town. The shrines of Manat and al-'Uzza in the neighbourhood were destroyed. Almost immediately, however, Muhammad had to face a serious military threat. A group of tribes hostile to the Meccans collected an army and moved against Mecca. Muhammad went out to meet them, accompanied by some 2,000 Meccans as well as his own troops, and after a hard-fought battle defeated them; this is the battle of Hunayn, which made him the strongest man in Arabia. Most of the Meccans now gradually became Muslims.

By this time, too, Muhammad's position in Medina was stronger, for the three main Jewish clans had been eliminated. When Muhammad first went to Medina, he expected that the Jews there would accept him as a prophet. When they failed to do so, and instead made hostile criticisms, his attitude changed. This was the underlying reason for the change of qibla in 624. Hitherto the Muslims had followed the Jews in facing Jerusalem in prayer, but now they turned round and faced Mecca instead. About April 624 a petty quarrel between a group of Muslims and Jews of the clan of Qaynuqa' became the ground for the expulsion of that clan from Medina. They had mainly been engaged in trading and also included smiths. A quarrel over blood-money led to the expulsion of the second clan of an-Nadir in August 625. The third clan, Qurayza, was involved in intrigues with the Meccans during the siege of Medina, and after the failure of the siege they were attacked and forced to surrender. One of their allies from Medina judged their case and decided that all the men should be executed and the women and children sold into slavery. After this there was no significant body of Jews in Medina, but there seem to have been small groups attached to various Arab clans and strictly subordinate to them. Later some large Jewish agricultural settlements outside Medina were brought under Muslim control and forced to pay a form of tribute. After the conquest of Mecca and the victory at Hunayn, Muhammad's personal authority was in fact very much greater, although there had been no change in the Constitution of Medina. He was, in Arab eyes, the chief of the clan of Emigrants and thus only one chief among several, though he also had some privileges as

Messenger of God. The clan of Emigrants, however, had now grown considerably as a result of further arrivals from Mecca, while nomads settling in Medina as confederates of Muhammad also seem to have been regarded as Emigrants. Already some nomadic tribes had become allies of Muhammad and presumably were regarded as members of his federation, and after Hunayn more did so. Because this was the situation, none of the chiefs of the clans of Medina was likely to offer serious opposition to Muhammad, so that his power was tending to become autocratic.

As more and more tribes or sections of tribes joined the federation, and relatively few tribes remained aloof, Muhammad and his chief lieutenants began to be aware of the problem this created, especially as it was becoming compulsory for those joining the federation to be Muslims. A normal activity of the nomads had been the razzia or raid aimed at driving off the camels of an unfriendly tribe; but Muslim tribes could not be allowed to raid one another. The Muslim leaders seem to have realized that the best way to avoid mutual razzias was to direct the energies of the tribesmen outwards towards Syria and Iraq. The largest of all the expeditions was one Muhammad himself led to a place called Tabuk near the gulf of Akaba (al-'Aqaba). He is said to have had 30,000 men, and it lasted from October to December 630. At the time of his death, another expedition was ready to set out towards Syria, and it did in fact do so despite the change in circumstances. This policy of expansion was vigorously pursued by the early caliphs.

Muhammad personally conducted the Hajj or Greater Pilgrimage in March 632, but after that his health declined and he died on 8 June 632.

2 THE POLITICAL HISTORY OF THE ISLAMIC WORLD

1. THE FORMATION OF THE CALIPHATE

The great political power which Muhammad had at his death was in part due to his prophethood and his own strong personality, but he was also technically regarded as chief of the clan of Meccan Emigrants within the federation of tribes constituting the Islamic polity. The most Muhammad had done to arrange for a successor to himself was to appoint Abu-Bakr to lead the formal worship when he was too ill to do so. After his death a meeting was held in Medina. The Helpers from Medina wanted their leading man, Sa'd ibn-'Ubada, to succeed to Muhammad's position, but this was strongly opposed by the Emigrants, who insisted that the nomadic tribes would not accept someone from Medina. Eventually it was agreed that Abu-Bakr should succeed to Muhammad's political position with the title of 'caliph' (*khalifa* meaning successor or deputy). He could not of course succeed to Muhammad's prophethood.

Abu-Bakr's rule lasted for only about two years, and for most of this time his chief concern was the subduing of revolts against the Islamic federation; some of these had begun before Muhammad's death. The revolts are collectively known as the wars of the Ridda or Apostasy, since they were given a religious colouring, though they seem to have been basically protests by nomadic tribes against giving tribute to Medina. The most serious rising was that in the Yamama, a district in the centre of Arabia well to the east of Mecca and Medina. This was led by a man called Musaylima, who claimed that he himself was a prophet on a level with Muhammad. He did indeed produce what he claimed were revelations from God with some religious content, but the religious aspect of the rising seems to have been subordinate to the political. This rising was eventually put down by a Muslim army led by Khalid ibn-al-Walid, one of the later Meccan converts to Islam, who is also known as 'the Sword of God'; but in the final battle there were numerous casualties on both sides. In another revolt in northern Arabia the leader was a woman, Sajda, who claimed to be a prophetess. At one point she is said to have tried to join forces with Musaylima, but nothing came of this and she was eventually defeated. There were somewhat similar movements in the Yemen and in eastern Arabia, but these too were finally defeated by Abu-Bakr's generals.

The period from Muhammad's death until 661 is known as that of 'the four rightly guided caliphs' or Rashidun. After Abu-Bakr the others were 'Umar (634–44), 'Uthman (644–56) and 'Ali (656–61). The caliphate then passed into the hands of Mu'awiya, a son of Abu-Sufyan, and the clan of Umayya managed to retain it among themselves until 750. They made Damascus their capital, and are known as the Umayyad dynasty. They were replaced by another Meccan family, known as the 'Abbasids, who were the descendants of Muhammad's uncle al-'Abbas. They moved the capital to Baghdad, but after the early tenth century lost all their political power, though they retained the title of caliph until 1258, when Baghdad was sacked by the Mongols. These political developments will be dealt with more fully in the third section of this chapter.

2. THE EXPANSION OF THE ISLAMIC STATE

For over a century after Muhammad's death the Islamic state continued to be essentially a federation of Arab tribes at least in theory. A non-Arab who became a Muslim was assigned to an Arab tribe as a client (*mawla*). Within the federation the caliph had special powers, and for a time these gradually increased.

Abu-Bakr and his successors fully understood the importance of diverting the energies of the nomads in an outward direction. Once the revolts of the Ridda had been quelled, these expeditions abroad became a regular occurrence, and assumed a more military character when they had to face the armies of the two empires, the Byzantine, which ruled Greater Syria and Egypt, and the Sassanian, which ruled Iraq and Iran. The rivalry between these two empires was centuries old. Frequent warfare between them in the second half of the sixth century had enabled the Meccan merchants to gain most of the trade between the Indian Ocean and the Mediterranean. In the early seventh century the Sassanians were proving superior and in 614 they captured Jerusalem and in 619 occupied Egypt. After about 622, however, under the emperor Heraclius, the Byzantines began to regain strength. By 627 Heraclius had become definitely the stronger, had recovered Egypt and Syria and was advancing into Iraq. In 628 the assassination of the Sassanian emperor Chosroes II was followed by dynastic disputes, and these led to the disintegration of the empire.

By this time, too, both empires were being challenged by the Muslims. In the course of their expeditions, the Muslims found themselves facing Byzantine and Sassanian armies, and a number of battles took place. Against the Byzantines the decisive battle took place in 636 at the River Yarmuk, a tributary of the Jordan, just south of the Sea of Galilee. In the next few years the

Muslims were able to occupy Syria up to the Taurus mountains, but despite frequent raids into Anatolia, this was for a time the limit of their territory. By 642 they had also expelled the Byzantines from Egypt. A Byzantine reoccupation of Alexandria in 645 was short-lived, and then the Muslims started moving westwards through North Africa. By about 649, too, they had established a strong fleet capable of beating the Byzantine navy.

Against the Sassanians there was a major victory for the Muslims at Qadisiyya, perhaps also in 636, and after that they gradually advanced eastwards. There was another important battle at Nihawand in Iran in 642, and after that Sassanian resistance collapsed, largely because the dynastic disputes had left no effective central administration. By about 652 the Muslims had extended their control over the whole of Iran, and later they moved on into central Asia and north-west India.

After the early raids, the men involved had returned to Medina, but as the raids went further and further afield this was felt to be a waste of time, and forward bases or camp cities were established, such as Basra and Kufa in Iraq and Cairouan in Tunisia; and in these the troops spent the winter periods between expeditions. Existing cities such as Damascus served a similar purpose. With the withdrawal of Byzantine power from Egypt and Syria and the collapse of the Sassanian empire, these forward bases became the centres of a provincial administration.

It must be emphasized that the chief purpose of the early expeditions was to gain booty, not to extend the Islamic religion by making converts or even to extend the Islamic state. Within Arabia some polytheistic tribes were given the choice of Islam or the sword, but elsewhere most of the inhabitants were Christians, Jews or others regarded as 'Peoples of the Book', and these received the status of 'protected minorities' (Ahl adh-Dhimma). This meant that, in line with traditional Arab ideas, they were regarded as weak tribes under the protection of the strong tribe of Muslims; and most governors saw such protection as a duty. In the new Islamic provinces, these minorities paid taxes to the governor, but the taxes were no more onerous than those they had previously paid to the empires. The individuals were, of course, in a sense second-class citizens and this led to some conversions; but the conversions were relatively few, except in Iran, where the traditional Zoroastrian religion had largely broken down and become little more than a department of government.

The expansion of the Islamic state stopped during the caliphate of 'Ali owing to internal troubles; but it began again once the Umayyads had established themselves, and continued at an even pace for most of the rest of their caliphate. The westward advance through North Africa eventually reached the Atlantic in Morocco. Then in 711 a force of Arabs and Berbers crossed into Spain, defeated the Visigothic king Roderick and were able to occupy all the chief towns of the Iberian peninsula, as well as Narbonne in France, which had been part of the Visigothic kingdom. There were further moves northwards, but an expedition into central France in 732 was defeated by King Charles Martel between Tours and Poitiers, and this marked the end of Muslim expansion in that direction, though Narbonne was retained until 759.

After the fall of the Umayyad dynasty in 750, an Umayyad prince managed to escape to Spain and under him Islamic Spain became a separate state not subject to the 'Abbasids in Baghdad. With the collapse of this Umayyad administration in 1031, the semi-independent Christian princelets in north-western Spain were able to commence what is known as the Reconquista, and in 1085 they reconquered Toledo. The Spanish Muslims now obtained support from two powerful North African dynasties, the

Almoravids and the Almohads, and it was not until the first half of the thirteenth century that the Christians were able to recapture Cordova and Seville. After this a small Islamic state continued to exist in Granada until 1492, when it was overwhelmed by the united kingdom of Aragon and Castile and Muslim presence in western Europe brought to an end. For a time there had also been a small Islamic state in Sicily.

It is appropriate at this point to say a word about the Crusades, since there is a slight connection of thought between these and the Spanish Reconquista. The original idea of the Crusades was to support the Byzantine empire against the Muslims, but they also came to mean, and to mean above all, the recovery of the Christian holy places in Palestine, so that Christian pilgrims could visit them freely. There was little interest in making converts. The first Crusade was proclaimed by the Pope in 1096, and this led to the establishment of small Christian states in Syria. There was a kingdom of Jerusalem until 1187, and Acre on the coast was held until 1291.

While the Crusades bulk large in Christian thinking, to the Muslims of the day they were no more than a minor frontier incident. At the time of the Christian invasion, the whole region was divided among several small Muslim rulers, at odds with one another. In one or two cases they joined with Christian groups against Muslim rivals. At this date the centre of Muslim power was hundreds of miles to the east of Iraq, and not much may have been known there about what was happening in Syria and Palestine.

By the time the 'Abbasids came to power in 750, the urge to expand had lessened, and such expansion as did continue to occur happened more slowly. There were also occasional withdrawals. Further expansion, too, was not always the result of raiding expeditions. For example, Muslim merchants trading in

West Africa across the Sahara would marry local women and establish families, which were brought up as Muslims. After a time some local African merchants would find it expedient to become Muslims, and occasionally also the local rulers. In this way Islam spread into the northern part of West Africa, though not to any extent into the regions nearer the coast.

Eastwards there was a developing Muslim presence in central Asia in places such as Bukhara and Samarkand, and this had varying fortunes. Under the Umayyads the Muslims had penetrated into north-western India as far as the Indus, and under the 'Abbasids they continued to advance and reached Bengal. The Hindus were accepted as protected minorities on the ground that the books of their philosophers could be interpreted as a form of monotheism.

3. THE CONTROL OF THE ISLAMIC STATE

The period of the four rightly guided caliphs is often regarded as an ideal time, when Islam was practised perfectly, but this is far from obvious when one looks at contemporary records. For one thing, three of the four caliphs were assassinated.

Abu-Bakr was succeeded by 'Umar, and it was under him that the expansion into Syria, Egypt and Iraq gained momentum. He also established an administrative system for the new provinces, and set up the Diwan, by which stipends were paid by the state to those serving in the armies. He was succeeded by 'Uthman from the clan of Umayya, who continued the expansion; but opposition to some of his policies led to his assassination in 656. 'Ali, Muhammad's cousin and son-in-law, was appointed successor; but his appointment was not wholeheartedly accepted. Muhammad's widow 'A'isha headed a revolt along with two senior Meccan Muslims, but 'Ali managed to defeat this force. He was also involved in hostilities with other dissident groups, above all that which was led by the governor of Syria, Mu'awiya, a son of Abu-Sufyan, who challenged 'Ali's appointment. After an indecisive battle at Siffin in 657 there was a partial truce and an attempt at arbitration which came to nothing. 'Ali, meanwhile, had his problems in Iraq and left Mu'awiya alone, and when he was assassinated in 661, Mu'awiya was generally accepted as caliph. Under him the Islamic state became stronger and was given a more definite shape, with Damascus as its capital.

After the death of Mu'awiya in 680 the clan of Umayya, the Umayyads, managed to keep the caliphate in their own hands until 750. In 683, however, 'Abd-Allah ibn az-Zubayr, son of one of 'A'isha's allies, claimed the caliphate and was supported by many of the Meccan Muslims. He had a considerable measure of success, especially in Arabia and Iraq, but was finally defeated in 692. This is known as the Second Civil War. The victor, the Umayyad 'Abd al-Malik (caliph 685–705), also further organized the caliphate. There were growing social problems, however, with which the Umayyads found it difficult to deal. The chief of these probably concerned the problem of the 'clients' or non-Arab Muslims, who resented being inferior to the Arabs. This seems to have been an important factor leading to the overthrow of the Umayyads by the 'Abbasids in 750. As descendants of Muhammad's uncle al-'Abbas, the 'Abbasids belonged to Muhammad's clan.

The power base of the 'Abbasids was more in the eastern provinces and they moved the central administration of the empire to Iraq, building the new capital of Baghdad. The earlier 'Abbasid caliphs were strong monarchs. The best known is Harun ar-Rashid (786–809). Difficulties were appearing, however, by the time of his son al-Ma'mun (813–33). To deal with these, al-Ma'mun set up the so-called Inquisition (*mihna*). By this, judges and people in similar positions were to state publicly that they believed in the createdness of the Qur'an and rejected the view that it was the uncreated word of God. This was not a piece of theological hair-splitting but an important socio-political question. From soon after the death of Muhammad, vaguely Shi'ite feelings had been widespread among the Muslims. The more precise forms will be studied in the later chapter on theology. At the time of al-Ma'mun, the general Shi'ite feeling took the form of a belief that the caliph was or should be a divinely inspired person whose decisions, because divinely inspired, would be binding on all Muslims. In other words, they wanted an autocracy; and this was also the standpoint of the caliphal officials. If the Qur'an, though it was God's word, was created, then it could presumably be changed by a leader inspired by God.

The opposite point of view was that of the 'ulama' or scholar-jurists, who had come to be an important class in Islam. They insisted that the Qur'an was the uncreated word of God and so something unchangeable, and that they alone were the authorized interpreters of it who could say how it was to be applied in contemporary situations. That implied that it was they and not the caliph and his officials who had the final word. The most notable opponent of al-Ma'mun's policy was Ahmad ibn-Hanbal, after whom the Hanbalite legal and theological school is named. He refused to say that he believed in the createdness of the Qur'an and was deprived of his office. The policy of the Inquisition was continued until about 850, when it was finally abandoned. This may have been mainly because it was failing to achieve the reconciliation of rival interests that had been hoped for. Its abandonment was tantamount to making the Sunnite form of Islam the official religion of the caliphate, and giving the 'ulama' an assured place in it.

In the later ninth century the power of the 'Abbasids began to decline. They had never been strong enough to assert their authority over Islamic Spain. Then a Shi'ite dynasty alleging descent from Muhammad's daughter Fatima, known as the Fatimids, occupied Tunisia and went on in 969 to conquer Egypt. These lands were taken out of nominal 'Abbasid control, since the Fatimids claimed that they were the rightful heads of the community of Muslims. Just as serious, however, was the inability of the 'Abbasids, with the forces at their command, to control their provincial governors. Some of these began to insist that they should be succeeded by sons or other relatives, and the caliphs were forced to acquiesce. This tendency was first seen in the more distant provinces, where in any case it was difficult for the caliphs to assert their authority; but it moved towards the centre. In 936 the general of the army of Iraq took over what remained of 'Abbasid power, and in 945 he was replaced by the dynasty of the Buyids or Buwayhids.

Although the 'Abbasid caliphs had thus no longer any political power, most of the new dynasties of governors found it useful to have the governors themselves nominally appointed by the caliphs, although the territory they actually ruled depended on what they could hold by force against their neighbours. Thus the caliphs, though without real power, retained a nominal headship of the Islamic community; and this continued until 1258, when Baghdad was sacked by a non-Muslim Mongol army and the 'Abbasids were killed or expelled.

From the ninth century onwards, Islamic history tends to become a history of dynasties. These are so numerous that it would be tedious here to mention them. At the centre of the caliphate the Buwayhids remained in control until 1055, when they were followed by a powerful Turkish dynasty, the Seljuqs, who retained power there until 1194. After that various dynasties shared power, and there was no strong dynasty at the centre when the Mongols invaded.

4. THE ISLAMIC WORLD AFTER THE 'ABBASIDS

After the withdrawal of the Almohad dynasty from Spain, the Christian Reconquista had made rapid progress, and with the fall of Seville in 1248 only the small kingdom of Granada in the south-east was left to the Muslims. This had been established in 1230 by the first of the Nasrid dynasty, and for two and a half centuries continued to have a measure of independence, though making payments of tribute to the Christians. In 1492, however, it was overpowered by the recently united kingdom of Aragon and Castile, and this ended the Islamic presence in Spain.

In North Africa the Almohads were becoming weaker, and in 1269 they lost all power and were replaced by several smaller dynasties. There was even less centralized control among the Muslim groups in West Africa. There the Muslims had not penetrated into the broad belt of tropical forest extending one or two hundred miles inland from the coast, but the area between that and the Sahara was predominantly Muslim, and continued through northern Nigeria into what is now the republic of the Sudan. The coast of East Africa as far south as Mozambique was also solidly Muslim.

In the central Islamic lands the outstanding fact was the rise and spread of the Ottoman Turks. Waves of Turks had been moving eastwards against the Byzantines and establishing small principalities in Anatolia. By the early fourteenth century the Ottomans had moved to the north-west of Anatolia and become leaders in the holy war against the Byzantines. Here they were joined by numerous other Turkish tribesmen eager to fight for their faith. This created a formidable military machine and also greatly increased the political power of the Ottoman rulers. In 1357 they were able to cross over into Europe at Gallipoli and then subdue much of the Balkans. The conquest of

Constantinople in 1453 was not a beginning but the end of the first phase of their European conquests. Constantinople became Istanbul and the seat of the Ottoman imperial government.

In the early sixteenth century the Ottomans were at the peak of their strength. They conquered Syria and Egypt, and gained a degree of control over Tunisia and Algeria. They also controlled Iraq and much of Arabia, and had a fleet in the Indian Ocean. In Europe they occupied Hungary and retained it for a century, but in 1528 an attempt to besiege Vienna failed. Gradually, however, the Ottoman empire declined and the European powers gained in strength. A second siege of Vienna in 1683 also failed, and from that point onwards the Ottomans were forced to withdraw from their European conquests, until in the post-First World War settlement of 1919 only European Turkey was left. By that settlement they also lost their Asian provinces and the nominal province of Egypt. The other North African provinces had already been lost. Out of the ruins of empire, however, the strong personality of Mustafa Kemal, supported by Turkish nationalist feeling, managed to create the Turkish republic as a secular state with its centre in Anatolia.

After the fall of Baghdad to the Mongols in 1258 the 'Abbasid caliphate came to an end, but a member of the 'Abbasid family who had escaped to Egypt claimed he was caliph, though it was only in Egypt that he was recognized. In the nineteenth century, however, the Ottoman sultans claimed that the caliphate had been transferred to them by the last of these Egyptian 'Abbasids, and this claim gained some recognition. The caliphate was formally abolished by the new Turkish republic in 1924 and has not been reconstituted.

The French invaded Egypt in 1798 as part of a move against European enemies in India, and the Ottoman general sent to expel them, Muhammad 'Ali (1769–1849), was by 1805 virtually the independent ruler of Egypt, though nominally subject to Istanbul. He had created a strong army on modern lines, and his descendants continued to rule Egypt until 1953; from 1867 they had the title of khedive and later that of king. Debts were incurred to various European powers, however, and from 1882, to ensure the repayment of these, a British force was stationed in Egypt and there was a British 'resident' with some political powers.

The Arabian peninsula has a complex history which it would be out of place to describe here in detail. From an early time, though with a gap from the fourteenth century to the sixteenth, much of the Yemen was ruled by an imam professing the Zaydite form of Shi'ism; but this rule was ended in 1962 when the Yemen People's Republic was proclaimed. In central Arabia, in 1930, the kingdom of Saudi (Su'udi) Arabia was formed, which aims at following Wahhabite principles and trying to ensure that its citizens live in accordance with the true, original Islam. This emphasis has communicated itself to other movements in the contemporary Islamic world.

In Iran a complete change occurred at the beginning of the sixteenth century. Shah Isma'il, the leader of what had originally been the Sufi order of the Safawiyya but had become a political force, conquered Azerbaijan in 1501, and then extended his control over the rest of Iran. At the same time he made the Imamite form of Shi'ism the official religion of his dominions; and since then Iran has been almost exclusively Imamite and the centre of this form of Islam. The Safavid dynasty, as it is called, continued to rule Iran until the early eighteenth century. Towards the end of that century, members of the Turkish tribe of Qajars gained supreme power and ruled Iran until 1924. In that year the commander-in-chief of the Iranian army managed to get himself appointed head of state as Riza Shah Pahlavi. The son who succeeded him was deposed in 1979, when Imam Khomeini proclaimed the Islamic Republic of Iran.

In Afghanistan and northern India the history of Islamic rule is again complex. There were numerous states of varying sizes under changing dynasties. The great achievement was the creation of the Mogul empire by Akbar the Great (d. 1605). In 1556 he came to the throne of a small state which included Delhi and Agra, but he rapidly expanded this into an empire comprising most of northern and central India. He was succeeded by a series of strong emperors – namely, Jihangir, Shah Jihan and Awrangzib, of whom the last, like Akbar, ruled for fifty years. On the death of Awrangzib in 1707, however, decline set in, and later emperors could do little to halt the growth of British colonial power. In 1858 the British deposed the last emperor for his involvement in the great Indian Mutiny, but for a decade or two before this the Moguls had had virtually no power. Hindus had been employed to a considerable extent in the administration of the empire, but at the same time Akbar and Awrangzib endeavoured to maintain its distinctive Islamic character.

Muslims also penetrated into the southern half of the Malay peninsula, into Indonesia, and into some islands of the Western Pacific; and most of these regions are now predominantly Muslim. As elsewhere in the Islamic world, the early history is complex. Eventually Malaysia and Indonesia became British and Dutch colonies respectively, gaining their independence in the mid-twentieth century. In terms of population, Indonesia is the largest Islamic state. On the Indonesian island of Java there was a high level of Islamic scholarship, and the schools there had close contacts with East African Islam.

3 THE TEACHING OF THE QUR'AN

1. THE TEXT OF THE QUR'AN

Most of the Qur'an was revealed to Muhammad in comparatively short passages. The longest continuous revelation is the story of Joseph in the Sura called after him, Surat Yusuf (12). At first the revelations were memorized by Muhammad and his followers, and parts at least were used in the formal worship. As time went on, many Muslims knew by heart large portions of the Qur'an. Muhammad himself did not write anything down, though latterly he used scribes; but some of his followers began to write down portions. Eventually, short revealed passages were brought together into suras or chapters. This operation was commenced by Muhammad himself, for the Qur'an has references to suras; but it seems to have been completed by later scholars in the time of the caliph 'Uthman.

When the Muslim armies moved into the neighbouring lands, problems arose with the repetition of parts of the Qur'an during the worship, since there were slight variations in what had been memorized. Finally, in about 653, the caliph 'Uthman commissioned a number of scholars, headed by Zayd ibn-Thabit, to produce a definitive text of the Qur'an. This is known as the collection of the Qur'an. The resulting version was written down and circulated throughout the empire, and all others were supposed to be destroyed. A century or two later some scholars found a few pre-'Uthmanic variants and listed them. By the early tenth century, however, it was found that there were some minor variants even within the 'Uthmanic text. These again were listed, but they were all held to be equally valid, and it was said that the Qur'an had been revealed in seven 'readings' (*qira'at*). What is now regarded as the standard form of the Qur'anic text is technically known as the reading of Hafs as reported by 'Asim.

Despite this mention of variants it should be realized that the text of the Qur'an is in very good condition compared with other books of that date. The variants are all very minor matters and make no difference to the essential teaching of the Qur'an. The good condition of the Qur'anic text is mainly due to the fact that the whole was revealed within twenty-five years, and this is in sharp contrast to the Old Testament, whose books came into existence over many centuries, and were often edited and re-edited to suit changing conditions. The suras are known as revealed either at Mecca or Medina, but sometimes a few verses from an earlier or later date have been included. A precise order of suras is indicated in the standard Egyptian edition produced in 1924, but this is questioned at numerous points by those Western scholars who have concerned themselves with questions of dating. In the nineteenth century Theodor Nöldeke divided the Meccan suras into three periods, and this seems to be roughly correct for the main parts of the suras. Further work on dating is to be found in Richard Bell's translation into English and in Régis Blachère's translation into French.

2. THE DOCTRINE OF GOD

Belief in God is at the centre of the Islamic religion. The first half of the short creed known as the Shahada is 'there is no deity but God'. The Arabic for this is *la ilaha illa Allah*; *ilah* denotes any god or deity, while *Allah* appears to be a contraction of *al-ilah*, 'the god', and so comparable to the Greek *ho theos*. Careful reading of the Qur'an shows that there were already people in Mecca who believed in Allah, but only as a 'high god' or superior deity along with others, even if he might be responsible for creation. This is clearly implied in one passage:

> If you ask them who created the heavens and the earth,
> and made the sun and moon subservient,
> they will certainly say, Allah . . .
> And if you ask them who sent down water from heaven
> and thereby revived the earth after its death,
> they will certainly say, Allah . . .
> And when they sail on the ship
> they pray to Allah as sole object of devotion,
> but when he has brought them safe to land
> they 'associate' [other deities with him].
>
> (29.61–5)

The word translated 'associate' comes from the same root as *shuraka*, which is frequently used in the Qur'an for the 'associates' or 'partners' the pagans give to God – that is, the other deities.

Another passage shows that there were people in Mecca who disbelieved in Muhammad's message, and yet had a high belief in Allah:

> Say, Whose is the earth and those in it . . .?
> They will say, Allah's.
> Say, Will you not be admonished?
> Say, Who is Lord of the seven heavens
> and Lord of the mighty throne?

They will say, Allah.
Say, Will you not fear him?
Say, In whose hand is the dominion of all things,
[so that] he gives protection
but no protection is given against him? . . .
They will say, Allah.
Say, How are you bewitched?

(23.84–9)

These people, or some of them, are further stated to regard the other deities to whom they pray as interceding with Allah on their behalf:

They worship apart from Allah what neither harms nor benefits them,
and they say, These are our intercessors with Allah.

(10.18; cf. 39.3)

These deities doubtless include the three mentioned in Sura 53, Allat, al-'Uzza and Manat, while others, presumably male, are named in connection with Noah (70.23), and seem to have been worshipped in southern Arabia. The following passage refers to female deities:

If you ask them who created the heavens and the earth,
they will certainly say, Allah.
Say, Do you then consider that what you call on apart
from Allah,
those [female beings] are able,
if Allah wills evil for me, to remove this evil,
or, if he wills mercy for me, to hold back this mercy?

(39.38)

(The pronouns and participles here are feminine.) It would further appear that these deities were thought of as angels:

> The angels, who are servants of the Merciful,
> they make females . . .
> They said, Had the Merciful willed,
> we would not have worshipped them.
> They have no knowledge of that; they only guess.
>
> (43.19f.)

The pagan deities were also sometimes thought of as sons or daughters of God (6.100). It was perhaps because the three female deities mentioned were worshipped in the neighbourhood of Mecca that there are verses which taunt the Arabs who set a high value on male descendants (see 16.58f.) with assigning only daughters to God while they have sons: 'Has your Lord then distinguished you [Arabs] with sons and taken for himself from the angels females?' (17.40; cf. 37.149f.).

All this material suggests that when Muhammad began to receive revelations there were many people in Mecca who believed in Allah as one deity among several, though superior to them. (This point is dealt with more fully in my *Muhammad's Mecca: History in the Qur'án* (Edinburgh: Edinburgh University Press, 1988), pp. 29–36.) This may have made it easier for some people to accept Muhammad's teaching, but it also meant that their outlook had to be corrected where it was faulty.

The denial of the existence of other deities, as in the first clause of the Shahada, is found explicitly in a verse where the unbelievers reject it and abuse Muhammad:

> Thus we deal with the wicked;
> for when it is said to them,

There is no deity but God,
they are arrogant and say,
Shall we abandon our deities for a mad poet?

(37.34–6)

The clause is also found in 47.19; and in other verses it occurs in the form 'There is no deity but he.'

The theme of God's goodness to his creation, and especially to human beings, is found early in the Qur'an, as was seen in a previous section. Two later passages expressing the same thought are the following:

Did you not see that God sends down rain from heaven
and the earth becomes green?
God is gracious, wise.
To him belongs whatever is in the heavens
and whatever is in the earth; and God is the Self-
sufficient, the Praiseworthy.
Did you not see that God made subservient to you
whatever is in the earth,
and the ship that sails on the sea by his command?
He holds back the heaven so that it does not fall
on the earth unless by his leave.
God is for people the Gracious, the Compassionate.
He it is who gives you life,
who causes you to die and gives you life [again].
People are indeed ungrateful.

(22.63–6)

God is he who created the heaven and the earth,
and sent down water from heaven,
producing fruits as sustenance for you;

he has made the ship subservient to you to sail on the sea
at his command;
and he has made the rivers subservient to you;
he has made subservient to you the sun and the moon as
they run their courses,
and he has made subservient to you the night and the day.

(14.32f.)

There are also many passages in the Qur'an which call people's
attention to the signs in nature of God's goodness. One such is:

A sign for them is the dead earth which we revive
and from which we bring forth grain;
and of that they eat.
We placed in it gardens of date-palms and vines,
and we caused springs [of water] to gush forth in it,
that they might eat of its fruit
and of what their hands have laboured at;
will they not give thanks?
Glory be to him who created all the pairs of what the
earth grows and of themselves,
and of what they know not.
A sign for them is the night;
we strip from it the day, and then they are in darkness.
The sun runs to a resting-place [appointed] for it . . .
For the moon we have decreed mansions
until it returns [looking] like an old [curled] palm-branch.
It is not fitting for the sun to overtake the moon,
nor is the night outstripping the day;
but each moves in an orbit.
Also a sign for them is that we bear their progeny on the
laden ship.

If we will, we drown them,
and there is no helper for them,
nor are they saved, unless as a mercy from us,
and enjoyment [of life] for a time.

(36.33–44)

Other shorter passages mention these and similar signs, including the creation of the heaven and the earth, the stability of the mountains, and the changing winds. The central thought in many of these passages is the goodness of this powerful God towards human beings. In return they are called upon to be grateful to him and worship him. After a passage praising God's goodness, there comes the verse: 'Of his signs is that he sends winds announcing [rain], so that you may taste of his mercy, and the ships may sail at his command, and you [in turn] may seek from his abundance; haply you will be thankful' (30.46).

There are also passages of a later date in which the beneficent power of God is contrasted with the powerlessness of the supposed deities of the pagans. An example of this is in a passage which, after speaking of angels being sent down by God to warn people that there is no deity but himself, continues:

He created the heaven and the earth in truth;
may he be exalted above what they associate [as deities
with him].
He created the human being from a drop [of seed];
and yet he is an open opponent.
The cattle too he created, from which you have warm
[clothing] and [other] advantages;
and from which you eat.
In them is credit for you when you drive them home [in the
evening]

and take them to pasture [in the morning].
They bear your loads to a land you could not reach
except with trouble to yourselves;
your Lord is gentle, compassionate.
Horses, mules and asses he creates that you may ride on them
and as an ornament; he also creates what is unknown to you.
It is for God to direct in the [right] way; but some turn
aside from it;
had he willed he would have guided you all.
It is he who sends down water from heaven for you;
from it [you] drink,
and from it are trees as pasture [for your herds].
By it he causes crops to grow for you,
and the olive, the date-palm, grapes and all kinds of fruit;
in that is a sign for those who reflect.
He has made of service to you the night and the day;
and the sun, moon and stars are subservient to you by his
command;
in that is a sign for people of understanding.
Also [of service] is what he has created for you in the
earth of different kinds;
in that is a sign for people who reflect.
He has made of service to you the sea
that you may eat fresh flesh [of fish] from it,
and take from it ornaments which you wear;
and you see ships ploughing in it
so that you [in trade] may seek of his abundance;
perhaps you will be thankful.
He has set in the earth firm [mountains],
lest it quake with you,
and rivers and roads;
perhaps you will be guided.

Is he who creates [all this] like him who does not
create [anything]?

(16.3–17)

The Qur'an accepts the belief that the world was created in six
days as in the book of Genesis; but it has only scattered references
to this (e.g. 32.4; 41.9f.). There is no detailed description of what
was done on each of the six days, as in the account at the
beginning of the Old Testament. Many Western Christians seem
to think that the work of creation was confined to these six days,
but this is not the view of the Old Testament. There creation is
regarded as a continuing process, and in particular each human
being is created individually by God. The passages quoted from
the Qur'an show that it also regards creation in this way.

The Qur'anic conception of the all-pervading creative activity
of God leads to statements that make it seem that the human will
is completely dominated by the divine will, and that what seem to
be human acts are really God's acts. There is a passage which
asserts that God was the real author of the victory in the battle of
Badr: 'You [Muslims] did not kill them [the enemy], but God
killed them, and you [Muhammad] did not shoot [the arrow]
when you shot, but God shot them' (8.17).

In particular, an individual's choice of belief or unbelief in the
revelations seems to depend on God:

This is a reminder, so that he who wills may choose
a way to his Lord;
but you will not so will, except it be that God wills.

(76.29f.; cf. 10.99f.; 74.56; 81.27–9)

The question of whether a person believes or not is often
connected with the idea of God's favour, help or guidance on the

one hand and that of his leading astray or abandonment on the other.

> If God wills to guide a man, he enlarges his breast for
> *islam* [or surrender to God], and if he wills to lead a
> man astray, he makes his breast narrow and contracted.
> (6.125)

> Had God willed he would have made you one
> community, but he leads astray whom he wills and
> guides whom he wills. (6.93)

> By this [simile God has coined] he leads astray many and
> by this he guides many; and he leads astray only the
> evildoers. (2.26)

The pre-Islamic Arabs thought that the main events in a person's life were predetermined by fate (or time), and the Qur'an seems to have accepted this idea but replaced fate by God. Thus it is said of Lot in 27.57: 'We delivered him and his household, except his wife whom we had predetermined to be of the lingerers.' As will be seen in a later chapter, God's decree (*qada'*) and predetermination (*qadar*) were much discussed by later theologians.

In the later years at Medina some Muslims complained to Muhammad if they suffered any misfortune, and he was told to say to them: 'Nothing will befall us except what God has written [decreed] for us' (9.51). A similar earlier verse is: 'No disaster occurs in the earth or in yourselves, unless it was in a book before we brought it about' (57.22).

Despite this apparent denial of human ability to do anything, the Qur'an insists that human beings are responsible for their acts. There are a number of verses which suggest that God's guidance, or alternatively his leading astray, follows on some decision of the individual.

Those who do not believe in God's signs, God does not
guide.   (16.104)

Truly I [God] am forgiving to him who repents and
believes and acts uprightly, and who also accepts
guidance.   (20.82)

How will God guide a people who disbelieved after
believing? . . .
God does not guide the wicked people.   (3.86)

Above all, human responsibility is implied in the doctrine of the Last Judgement, since the Qur'an also holds that God is just, and it would obviously be unjust to punish someone for an act for which he was not responsible. The doctrine was present in the Qur'anic revelations from the beginning (as was noted above). On the Last Day, human beings will be raised from the dead and brought before God to be judged, and the judgement will be based on the goodness or badness of their acts. They will then be assigned either to the Garden or the Fire – that is, to Paradise or to hell. Sometimes it is said that their acts will be weighed in a balance.

As for him whose balances are heavy [with good acts],
he shall be in a pleasing life.
As for him whose balances are light,
his mother [that is, dwelling] shall be the pit;
and what informs you what this is? –
a raging fire.[1]   (101.6–11)

---

[1]   This follows traditional Muslim interpretations of a difficult passage.

The final state of the good and the wicked is sometimes described more fully, as in the following passage:

> Friends on that day shall be enemies to one another,
> except the pious.
> O my servants, there is no fear over you this day,
> and you are not grieved,
> you who believed in our signs and were surrendered [as
> Muslims].
> Enter the Garden, you and your wives, in great joy.
> Golden trays are brought round for them and goblets
> containing what their souls desire and what delights the
> eyes;
> and you shall be there everlastingly.
> This is the Garden which you inherit [as reward] for what
> you were doing.
> Therein you have abundant fruit from which to eat.
> The wicked are in the torment of hell everlastingly.
> It will not be lightened for them, and they are in despair
> there.
> We did not wrong them,
> but it was they who were wrongdoers.
> They cried [to a guard], O sir,
> let your Lord put an end to us;
> [but] he said, You are remaining [here].
> We once brought you the truth;
> but most of you were turning away from the truth.
>
> (43.67–78)

This passage makes it clear that Muslim women have a place in Paradise, and there are other passages (e.g. 13.23) which speak of men, women and children entering as families. Formerly, Western accounts of Islam made much of the dark-eyed houris who were to be the companions of the believers there (44.54; 52.20; 55.72; 56.23). In other passages (e.g. 37.48), there are descriptions of the delightful female companions of the blessed, but without their being called houris.

In considering these accounts of life in Paradise, it is important to remember that they are attempts to express in human language something which the human mind cannot fully comprehend. This means too that there is no point in trying to harmonize completely different descriptions of life in Paradise, since they are merely the nearest the human mind can come to an adequate conception. It may also be noted that many later Muslims took the view that the greatest of the joys of Paradise would be the vision of God; and for this they found justification in the Qur'an: 'Faces that day will be bright, looking to their Lord' (75.22f.).

There are also some verses in the Qur'an which ascribe to God 'the most beautiful names' (7.180; 17.110; 20.8; 59.24), and of course many names are given to him, especially at the ends of verses. Later Muslims took over the general idea and produced a list of the ninety-nine most beautiful names, making this the basis of a form of meditation using the *subha* or rosary. The names themselves come from the Qur'an, where there are many verses ending with two names of God, as can be seen in passages quoted above; and in fact more than ninety-nine names can be found.

3. PROPHETHOOD

While in the earliest passages of the Qur'an the vocation of Muhammad is said to be that of a 'warner' (of the Last Judgement) or 'one who reminds', he soon came to be spoken of as a prophet or messenger, and among Muslims the most usual way of referring to him is as 'the messenger of God'. Some later Muslim scholars distinguished the functions of the prophet and the messenger: a prophet was anyone who had received a message from God, whereas the messenger was one who had been commissioned by God to take messages to a particular people; and it was then said that there had been 124,000 prophets but only 315 messengers. These numbers are fanciful, and are not justified by anything in the Qur'an, though the Arabic word for messenger indicates someone sent. In the case of both the prophet and the messenger, the initiative came from God. Since the word 'messenger' in English has no special religious connotations, it is best to speak of Muhammad's vocation as a call to be a prophet.

When the Meccans expressed disbelief in Muhammad's prophethood, the Qur'an insisted that he followed on a long line of prophets in earlier times and in different places. It was implied that all these had proclaimed the same essential message from God and had called on people to believe in God and in the judgement on the Last Day, when they would be assigned to Paradise or hell according to their acts. It was also implied that all these previous prophets had had the same task of proclaiming this message to people who had no belief in God. The Qur'an shows no knowledge of the book-prophets of the Old Testament, whose function was to criticize people who had a belief in God but were deviating from this and were disobeying his commands, and to warn these people of punishment.

The Qur'an has accounts of a number of previous prophets, and these serve to reinforce the point that Muhammad was following in a long tradition. This may be illustrated by one of the accounts of Abraham:

Relate to them the story of Abraham,
when he said to his father and his people,
What do you worship?
They said, We worship idols,
and to them we constantly cleave.
He said, Do they hear when you call,
or profit you or harm?
They said, Nay, we found our fathers acting thus.
He said, Have you considered what you have been
worshipping,
you and your fathers of old?
They are an enemy to me – except the Lord of the worlds,
who created me and who guides me,
who gives me to eat and to drink,
and when I am ill heals me,
who causes me to die, then brings me to life [again],
and who, I hope, will forgive my sins on the Day of
Judgement.
My Lord, give me wisdom,
and write me with the upright,
and grant me a good report among later generations,
and set me among those who inherit the Garden of
Delight.
Forgive my father, for he was among the erring,
and put me not to shame on the day when we are raised
up;
the day when neither wealth nor sons profit [anyone]
except him who comes to God with a sound heart;
[the day] when hell shall appear plainly to the erring.
It will be said to them,
Where is what you have been worshipping apart from
God?

Do they deliver you, or do they deliver themselves?
They will be thrown into [hell],
they and [those] seduced,
they and the hosts of Iblis altogether.
The [seduced] will say, disputing [with their false gods],
By God, we were indeed in clear error
when we made you equal with the Lord of the worlds.
It was only the wicked who led us astray.
So we have no witnesses and no warm friend.
Would that we might have [another] turn [on earth],
that we might be among the believers.

(26.69–102)

A shorter account of Abraham's prophethood is the following:

Mention in the Book Abraham;
he was upright, a prophet.
When he said, O my father, why do you worship what
hears not and sees not and benefits you nought?
O my father, knowledge has come to me that has not
come to you,
so follow me and I will lead you in a straight path.
O my father, do not worship Satan;
Satan is a rebel against the Merciful.
O my father, I fear lest a punishment from the Merciful
come upon you,
and you become a companion of Satan.
[His father] said, Are you turning away from my gods,
Abraham
If you do not desist, I shall surely stone you;
so leave me for a long while.
[Abraham] said, Peace be upon you.

I shall ask my Lord to forgive you;
he has been gracious to me.
I shall withdraw from you and from what you pray to
apart from God,
and I shall pray to my Lord;
perhaps in my prayer to my Lord I shall not be unheard.
When he had withdrawn from them and from what they
were worshipping apart from God,
we gave him Isaac and Jacob, and made each of them a
prophet.

(19.41–9)

An account is also given of how at one point Abraham believed
that God was calling on him to sacrifice his son, and he set about
doing so but was stopped by God (37.101–11). In this passage the
son is not named, and it is generally held by Muslims that the son
in question was Ishmael and not Isaac as in the Bible. The Qur'an
also speaks of Abraham as praying at Mecca, and along with
Ishmael establishing the Ka'ba as a place for the worship of God
(2.125–9; cf. 22.26–31). A section of the Arabs of Muhammad's
time accepted Ishmael as their ancestor.

Another function of the Qur'anic accounts of prophets was to
show how those who rejected the prophet's message were
punished, while the prophet and the believers were saved. Noah
was an example of this:

The people of Noah counted false the messengers.
When their brother Noah said to them,
Will you not fear [God]?
I am a faithful messenger to you;
so fear God and obey me.
I ask you for no reward for this;

my reward is [a matter] only for the Lord of the worlds;
so fear God and obey me.
They said, Shall we believe you,
when [only] the most abject follow you?
He said, I have no knowledge of what they have been
doing.
Their reckoning is for my Lord alone,
if you understand.
I am not one who turns away the believers;
I am only a clear warner.
They said, Unless you desist, Noah,
you will be of those stoned.
He said, My Lord, my people count me a liar.
So judge decisively between me and them,
and save me and those with me of the believers.
We saved him and those who were with him in the laden
ship [ark] and afterwards we drowned the rest.
Surely in that there is a sign, but most of them are not
believing.

(26.105–20)

This account is followed by accounts in very similar words of
three Arabian prophets not mentioned in the Bible and of
Abraham's nephew Lot. The three Arabian prophets are Hud,
sent to the tribe of 'Ad; Salih, sent to the tribe of Thamud; and
Shu'ayb, sent to the people of the grove (perhaps the
Midianites). In each case the prophet's message was rejected
and the people were punished, though in different ways. The
account of Lot may be quoted as an example of the treatment of
these prophets; it makes use of the destruction of Sodom and
Gomorrah as told in the Bible, though without naming the
towns:

The people of Lot counted false the messengers.
When their brother Lot said to them,
Will you not fear [God]?
I am a faithful messenger to you;
so fear God and obey me.
I ask you for no reward for this;
my reward is [a matter] only for the Lord of the worlds.
Do you come at the males of the worlds,
and leave your wives, whom your Lord created for you?
You are indeed a people who transgress.
They said, Unless you desist, Lot, you will be of those
expelled
He said, I am of those who abhor what you do.
My Lord, save me and my family from what they are
doing.
So we saved him and his family all together,
except an old woman [who was] among those who
remained;
then we destroyed the others and rained upon them a
rain;
bad was the rain of those warned.
Surely in this there is a sign; but most of them were not
believing.

(26.160–74)

At various points there are lists of Biblical personages whom the Qur'an regards as prophets. The longest is: 'We made revelations to you [Muhammad] as we made revelations to Noah and the prophets after him; and we made revelations to Abraham, Ishmael, Isaac, Jacob and the Patriarchs, and to Jesus, Job, Jonah, Aaron, Solomon; and we gave David the Psalms' (4.163). Another list (in 6.84–6) mentions several of these and also Joseph, Moses,

Zechariah, John (the Baptist), Elias (or Elijah) and Lot. It is also held that all these prophets proclaimed the same message in essentials.

> Say [Muslims], we believe in God and in what was sent
> down [revealed] to us, and in what was sent down to
> Abraham, Ishmael, Isaac, Jacob and the Patriarchs,
> and in what was given to Moses and Jesus,
> and in what was given to the prophets from their Lord;
> we make no distinction between any of them;
> and to [God] we are submitted [as Muslims].
>
> (2.136)

There is a great wealth of material in the Qur'an about Moses. There are some references to his birth and early life, to his call from the burning bush and to his association with Aaron; he is also said to have received Scriptures from God. The primary purpose of his prophethood, however, is the calling of Pharaoh and his people to belief in God; and there are many accounts of his arguments with the magicians. The drowning of the Egyptians in the sea is then seen as their punishment for rejecting their prophet, and comparable to the punishments of other unbelieving peoples. The plagues which afflicted them are also seen as a punishment, but partly for refusing to let the Israelites leave Egypt (7.130–6). Moses had already asked Pharaoh to let the Israelites go with him (7.105, 134; cf. 26.17).

Moses is further said to have been told by God to take his servants away by night and then lead them across the sea (7.138; cf. 10.90). There is some account of the Israelites at the mountain (Sinai or Horeb), and of Moses spending forty nights on the mountain with God and receiving laws, while in his absence a mysterious person called as-Samiri made a calf which the people worshipped (7.142–56). In another passage (5.20–6) Moses is said to have called on the Israelites to enter a holy land, but they refused because they were afraid of the people living there, and they were then made to spend forty years in the wilderness. Elsewhere, however, without any reference to this, God is said, after the drowning of the Egyptians, to have made the despised people inherit the eastern and western parts of a land blessed by him (7.137). For those familiar with the Biblical account of Moses, it is not too difficult to piece this material together. From the Qur'an alone, however, it would be virtually impossible; and for this reason later Muslim scholars went to the Old Testament and gave a more connected account of the work of Moses.

The Qur'anic conception of prophethood is thus essentially a generalization, based on what Muhammad had experienced and then actually achieved. The prophet is one to whom God has spoken and who responds by calling on his people to believe in God and the Last Judgement; and he himself and those who accept his message are preserved by God, while those who reject his message are punished. This is succinctly expressed in a verse placed between accounts of Noah and Moses.

> Then we sent our messengers one after other.
> When to its community its messenger came,
> they counted him false;
> so we called them to follow one the other [to disaster].
>
> (23.44)

At one point Muhammad is called 'the seal of the prophets' (33.40). To the first hearers this probably meant no more than that the revelations to Muhammad confirmed those to previous prophets. At one point, which might have been in Muhammad's lifetime but perhaps was only later, this was taken to mean that Muhammad was the last of the prophets, after whom there would be no other. When in the first Islamic century Muslim scholars developed the doctrine of the corruption of the Jewish and Christian Scriptures (as will be explained in the next section), this phrase was taken to mean that Muhammad was the final prophet, correcting the errors that had crept into previous revelations, and giving the full and perfect version of God's revelation to humanity. Christians would probably be ready to agree that there is unlikely to be any further prophet inaugurating a new major religion; but they would hold that God may reveal to believing individuals ways of dealing with specific new problems arising from the changes taking place in the world.

4. OTHER RELIGIONS

Muhammad and his early followers certainly knew of the existence of the Jewish and Christian religions and were in touch with many members of them, but they had probably had few close contacts with any until they had to deal with the Jewish clans in Medina. These facts help to explain the original acceptance of Jews and Christians as fellow believers.

> Those who believe [as Muslims] and those who are Jews,
> and the Christians and the Sabians,
> whoever believes in God and the Last Day and acts uprightly,
> they have their reward from their Lord.
>
> (2.62)

A verse revealed soon after the Hijra still speaks favourably of the Christians, though not of the Jews:

> You [Muhammad] will indeed find the most hostile of people

to the believers are the Jews and the idolaters.
You will indeed find the closest in love to the believers
are those who say, We are Christians.
That is because there are among them priests and
monks,
and they are not proud.

(5.82)

Another favourable account of the Christians, perhaps a little
later in date, is the following:

We gave Jesus the Gospel
and in the hearts of followers set kindness and mercy,
and the monastic state, but that they invented –
we did not prescribe it for them –
[it was] only out of a desire to please God,
but they did not observe it aright.

(57.27)

There is at least one favourable early account of the Jews:

God made a covenant with the Israelites . . .
and God said, I am with you;
if you observe the Worship and pay the Alms,
and believe my messengers and support them,
and give God a good loan, I shall remit your sins,
and bring you to Gardens through which rivers flow.
Whoever of you disbelieves after that has erred from the
way.
So for their breaking their covenant
we have cursed them and hardened their heart.

(5.12f.; cf. 5.44)

By the Israelites here, however, it is possible that only those from the time of Moses onwards are intended, for another passage, after speaking approvingly of Abraham, Isaac and Jacob, goes on to say, 'that is a community which has passed away' (2.134).

In Muhammad's later years the Jews of Medina, and occasionally also some Christians, would criticize various statements in the Qur'an about Biblical figures. As has been seen, there were many references to such persons, and some of the stories differed appreciably from the Bible. In certain cases, but by no means in all, the variations are now known to come from Jewish books other than the Bible. This critical attitude towards the Jews led to less favourable statements in the Qur'an about them. One such is:

> Of the Jews some alter the words from their sets,
> and they say, We hear and disobey,
> and, Hear something not heard, and, Show regard for us,
> twisting their tongues and slandering the religion.
> If they had said, We hear and obey, and, Hear, and,
> Consider us,
> it would have been better for them and more correct.
> But God cursed them for their unbelief,
> so that except for a few they do not believe.
>
> (4.46f.; cf. 2.75; 5.13, 41)

The vague phrase 'alter the words from their sets' has been used because the precise meaning of the Arabic is not clear. The word translated 'sets' can mean either 'places' or 'meanings' and the word translated 'alter' is the verb from which comes the noun *tahrif*, used when speaking of the 'corruption' of the Scriptures. Thus it is not clear whether the Qur'an is accusing the Jews of altering the text of their Scripture or merely of altering the interpretation. It has been suggested by Western scholars that the first part of the verse means that the Jews were playing verbal tricks on the Muslims, and in particular were making use of the similarity in sound between the Hebrew *shama'nu wa-'asinu*, 'We hear and obey', and the Arabic *sami'na wa-'asayna*, 'We hear and disobey.' This verse and some similar verses were used by Muslim scholars in the century after Muhammad's death to justify their doctrine of the complete corruption of the Jewish and Christian Scriptures; but the verses by themselves do not assert thorough-going corruption either of the texts or of the interpretations. On one or two occasions there may have been attempts to conceal verses which the Muslims claimed foretold the prophethood of Muhammad. Despite the slightness of the Qur'anic basis for the doctrine, it was generally accepted by Muslims. In the new provinces it greatly helped the more simple-minded Muslims in arguments with educated Christians, for they could refuse to accept anything based on the Bible.

There is relatively little in the Qur'an from the New Testament. There is an account of the miraculous birth of John the Baptist and above all there is an account of the virginal conception and birth of Jesus. Since this is relevant to Muslim–Christian dialogue, it is worth quoting it in full. It will be seen that, while the account of the conception is similar to that in the New Testament, the description of the birth is different.

Mention in the Book Mary,
when she withdrew from her people to an easterly place.
She took in front of them a curtain;
then we sent to her our Spirit,
who appeared to her as a handsome person.
She said, I take refuge with the Merciful from you if you
fear [God].

He said, I am only the messenger of your Lord to give
you a pure boy.
She said, How shall I have a boy,
when no man touched me and I was not wanton?
He said, Thus [shall it be]; your Lord said,
It is easy for me, and [it is] that we may make him
a sign for the people and a mercy from us.
It is a thing decided. So she conceived him,
and withdrew with him to a far place,
and the birth-pangs drove to the trunk of a palm;
she said, Would I had died before this,
and been in oblivion, forgotten.
Then he called her from beneath her, Grieve not;
your Lord has set beneath you a stream.
Shake towards you the trunk of the palm,
and it will drop moist, ripe [dates] upon you.
So eat and drink and be of good cheer,
and if you see any person, say,
I have vowed to the Merciful a fast,
and today I speak to nobody.
She brought him to her people carrying him.
They said, O Mary, you have done a thing unheard of.
O sister of Aaron, your father was not an evil man,
nor your mother wanton.
She pointed to him; they said,
How shall we speak with one in the cradle, a child?
He said, I am God's servant;
he has given me the Book and made me a prophet.
He has made me blessed wherever I am,
and has enjoined on me the Worship and Alms,
so long as I live, and [to be] dutiful to my mother;
and has not made me oppressive, impious.

Peace is on me the day I was born, the day I shall die,
and the day I shall be raised alive.
That is Jesus, son of Mary –
the statement of the truth of which there is no doubt.
(19.16–34).

After this glance at some of the things the Qur'an says about Judaism and Christianity, there is a further important point to be made. A Jew or Christian reading the Qur'an, and finding so many Biblical persons referred to, tends to think that this shows a wide familiarity with the two religions. Careful examination, however, shows that the opposite is the case. Despite the numerous Biblical figures mentioned, the Qur'an shows remarkably little knowledge of the essentials of the Jewish and Christian religions other than belief in God and the Last Judgement. In respect of Judaism there is nothing about God's call to Abraham to leave his homeland, and no appreciation of the fact that the primary work of Moses was to bring his people out of Egypt and successfully lead them through the wilderness to the land promised to Abraham. There is no realization that David was primarily a successful war-leader who established a powerful kingdom, and no knowledge of the division of the kingdom into two, or of the exile and restoration.

There is virtually no knowledge of Christianity apart from the variant account of the virginal conception and birth of Jesus. There is also a verse (4.157) which apparently denies the death of Jesus on the cross, and others which speak of Christians worshipping three gods, sometimes apparently the Father, Jesus and Mary. This last is of course denounced, but it should be noted that this is tritheism and not the Christian doctrine of the Trinity, and that Christians also reject tritheism. It is possible, of course, that some of the Christians met by the early Muslims were not well instructed and held something similar to the beliefs stated in the Qur'an. A corollary of this fact of the relative ignorance of the Qur'an of Judaism and Christianity is that, as mentioned earlier, it strengthens the argument for holding that the Qur'an was directly revealed by God to Muhammad, since it contains so much truth about the being and nature of God.

It is worth saying a little more about the apparent denial of the Crucifixion, since this is very relevant to future Muslim–Christian relations. The belief that Jesus died on the cross and then on the third day was raised by God to eternal life (not merely resuscitated) is at the heart of the Christian faith. The central act of Christian worship is the Eucharist or Mass or Lord's Supper, and this commemorates the redeeming death of Jesus. The Qur'anic verse is somewhat vague. A possible translation is: 'They [the Jews] did not kill him, they did not crucify him, but it was made to seem to them.' The primary purpose of this verse is to deny that the Crucifixion was a Jewish victory, and with this Christians can agree; but they cannot possibly acquiesce in the assertion that the death on the cross did not happen. For future relations between Islam and Christianity, it is important that some other interpretation of the verse should be found which does not deny the central point of Christian belief. Attempts to do this are being made by some Muslim scholars, notably Mahmoud Ayoub in an article entitled 'The Death of Jesus: Reality or Delusion' (*Muslim World*, lxx, 1980, pp. 91–121). The final words of this article are worth quoting:

> The reproach of the Jews, 'for their saying, "We have surely killed Jesus the Christ, the son of Mary, the apostle of God,"' with which the verse starts, is not directed at the telling of a historical lie, or at the making of a false report. It is rather, as

is clear from the context, directed at human arrogance and folly, at an attitude towards God and His messenger. The words identifying Jesus are especially significant. They wished to kill Jesus, the innocent man, who is also the Christ, the Word, and God's representative among them. By identifying Christ in this context, the Qur'an is addressing not only the people who could have killed yet another prophet, but all of humanity is told who Jesus is.

The Qur'an is not here speaking about a man, righteous and wronged though he may be, but about the Word of God who was sent to earth and returned to God. Thus the denial of the killing of Jesus is a denial of the power of men to vanquish and destroy the divine Word, which is for ever victorious. Hence the words, 'They did not kill him, nor did they crucify him', go far deeper than the events of ephemeral human history; they penetrate the heart and conscience of human beings. The claim of humanity (here exemplified in the Jewish society of Christ's earthly existence) to have this power against God can only be an illusion. 'They did not slay him . . . but it seemed so to them.' They only imagined doing so.

In the last year or two of Muhammad's life the Muslims had more contacts with Jews and also some with Christians, and the Qur'an gives instructions about how to answer some of their attacks on Islam. The central point of Qur'anic apologetics was the development of the doctrine of 'the religion of Abraham'. It was insisted that Abraham was neither a Jew nor a Christian; and this is in a strict sense true, although they regarded him as their spiritual ancestor.

O People of the Book, why do you argue about Abraham?

The Torah and the Gospel were not revealed until after
him;
will you not be reasonable . . .
Abraham was neither a Jew nor a Christian;
but he was a *hanif*, a Muslim, and not one of the idolaters.

(3.65, 67)

When Jews and Christians tried to convert Muslims, Muhammad
was told to reply on behalf of his community that they belonged
to the religion of Abraham.

They say, Be Jews or Christians, and you will be guided.
Say [to them], No, but the religion of Abraham as a *hanif*,
and he was not of the idolaters.

(2.135)

The religion of Abraham is thus presented as a form of
monotheism other than Judaism and Christianity. In the Qur'an
the term *hanif* is applied primarily to Abraham, although in one
verse (30.30) Muhammad is told to direct his face towards the
religion as a Hanif, without any mention of Abraham. Muslim
scholars named one or two predecessors of Muhammad whom
they said were Hanifs, but there is no evidence that these persons
used the word of themselves. There are some variant readings of
Qur'anic texts which suggest that for a time a follower of
Muhammad may have been called a Hanif and his religion the
Hanifiyya.

5. THE FIVE PILLARS

The five chief religious duties of Muslims are commonly known as
the five pillars. In the Qur'an Muhammad received the basic

instructions about these, but elaborations in the practices occurred in his lifetime and later, and then jurists did much work on formulating the rules.

i. The Shahada or Profession of Faith

It is convenient to retain the word Shahada in English because of its preciseness. The Arabic word means 'witnessing', and the actual words of the Shahada are often prefixed by the phrase 'I bear witness that . . .'. The Shahada is a short creed and runs: 'There is no deity but God, Muhammad is the messenger of God.' The first phrase is found exactly in the Qur'an in 37.35 and 47.19, and in slightly varied form in other verses. The exact second phrase occurs in 48.29, but the idea is present throughout. The Shahada is sometimes used in the course of worship, and in this way is comparable to the creeds used in Christian worship. Longer creeds do exist in Islam, but they express the beliefs of individuals or schools, and none is officially accepted by the whole of Sunnite Islam.

ii. Salat or Formal Worship

The Arabic word *salat* is often translated 'prayer' or 'prayers', but 'formal worship' would be better, since much more is included than what is commonly understood by prayer in English. As well as words there are actions, and many of the words are not making requests but praising God. One verse (73.20) bids Muslims observe the Salat, and others (e.g. 2.238; 11.114; 17.78; 20. 139; 30.17; 50.39f.) indicate appropriate times, though there is no clear statement of what came to be accepted as the five obligatory times of worship. These are: before sunrise, noon, afternoon, sunset and evening. Supererogatory acts of worship may also be performed at other times. While at Mecca Muhammad and some of his followers rose during the night for meditation on the Qur'an and other devotions (73.1–4), but this was abrogated (73.20) after he went to Medina and had heavier daytime responsibilities.

The Salat is mostly performed by large numbers of Muslims together, but it may also be performed by individuals in isolation. In all cases the Salat is preceded by ablutions so that the worshipper is ritually pure. Performance in the mosque is not compulsory but is recommended, especially for the Friday noon worship, at which there is usually a sermon. Outside the mosque the worshipper normally spreads a prayer-carpet for himself to ensure ritual purity. Those engaging in the Salat must face in the direction of Mecca, the qibla. If a number are worshipping together, one stands in front as leader, while the others stand in rows behind. This leader gives the timing of the actions so that they are all made in unison; but leadership is not restricted to a special clerical class. For the obligatory times of worship the faithful are summoned by a muezzin or crier calling from the minaret of a mosque. Public participation in the Salat tends to be predominantly for men in the older Islamic countries. In some mosques there is a separate section for women; in others, if they are present, they have to remain behind the men. On the other hand, in some African countries there is little segregation of women, even for ablutions.

The Salat may be most simply described as consisting of an introduction, two or four 'cycles' according to the time of day, and a conclusion. To begin with the worshipper stands upright. Then, raising his hands to the level of his ears, he says the ascription of greatness (*takbir*) – that is, the words 'God is great [or greater].' This is followed by the recitation of the Fatiha, the opening sura of the Qur'an:

In the name of God, the Merciful, the Compassionate.
Praise be to God, the Lord of the worlds,
the Merciful, the Compassionate,
Lord of the Day of Judgement.
You we worship and you we entreat;
lead us in the straight way,
the way of those you have favoured,
not of those with whom you are angry, nor of the erring.

The introduction is completed by the recitation of one or more suras of the Qur'an.

The first 'cycle' (rak'a) begins with another ascription of greatness and then the bowing. For this the worshipper bends forwards with his hands on his knees. Then, after a brief return to the upright position, he prostrates himself – that is, kneels down and touches the ground with his forehead – at the same time making another ascription of greatness. After this first prostration, he sits briefly on his left foot and then makes a second prostration. This completes the first cycle. Then he stands up for the bowing which will begin the second cycle and repeats all this if there are further cycles. After the final cycle, however, he remains sitting on his left foot and repeats the Shahada. Then he says, 'Peace be upon you', first to the person on his right, then to the person on his left.

This is the basic framework of the Salat. Various pious expressions are widely used at certain points, and writers such as al-Ghazali encourage the devout Muslim to use many more. Al-Ghazali devoted one of the forty books of his *Revival of the Religious Sciences* to the Salat, and this is available in Edwin E. Calverley's *Worship in Islam*, with a full introduction explaining all the details. A shorter account of the Salat by al-Ghazali will be found in my *Faith and Practice of Al-Ghazálí* (pp. 130–6).

The Arabic word for petitionary or intercessory prayer is *du'a*, and this also is commended in the Qur'an. Abraham is reported as saying:

> My Lord, make me one performing the Salat, and [also] some of my posterity, O our Lord; and accept my Du'a.
>
> (14.40)

In another verse (19.48, quoted above) Abraham says that he will pray to God for his father and has hopes that his Du'a will be answered. There is also a verse (2.186) where God says he will answer the prayer of the one who prays.

iii. Almsgiving

In the Qur'an the performing of the Salat is often coupled with the paying of the *zakat*. This Arabic word is sometimes translated as 'legal alms' or 'poor tax', and these words give some idea of what it is, but not a complete one. It consists of the payment of a tenth or some other proportion of one's fruit and other crops, and also of a proportion of one's herds of camels and other animals, of one's gold and silver and of certain other forms of property. In some Islamic countries in later centuries this became a kind of state tax, which could be justified by the fact that in Muhammad's later years most of it was paid to him and then distributed by him to help the poor and for various political purposes. Some of the derivatives of the Arabic root *zaka*, however, suggest purification, and to begin with there was some idea that the giving of Zakat was a purification of the giver.

The requirement of paying Zakat was introduced at some point after the Hijra. At first its chief purpose may have been to detach individual Muslims from undue attachment to worldly wealth. When various tribes which had been hostile to Islam changed their minds and became allies, the Muslims were told that 'if they perform the Salat and give the Zakat, they are your brothers in religion' (9.11; cf. v. 5). The payment of Zakat was not unsurprisingly disliked by the tribes, and was one of the causes of the wars of apostasy with which Abu-Bakr had to deal. The Qur'an justified it as an element in the common religion of the People of the Book (98.5), and also included it in the covenant God made with the Israelites (2.83; *passim*).

iv. The Fast of Ramadan

The observation of the month of Ramadan as one of fasting is based on the following passage:

> O you who believe, fasting is prescribed for you as it was for those before you, that you may reverence [God]. [Fast] a certain number of days; he of you who is sick or on a journey [shall fast] a similar number of other days . . . [Fast for] the month of Ramadan in which the Qur'an was sent down as guidance for the people and as clear proofs of the guidance and the Furqan. Whoever of you who is present [at home] during the month, let him fast [throughout] it; whoever of you is sick or on a journey [shall fast a similar] number of other days. God wants [to make things] easy for you; he does not want to make [them] difficult; he wants you to complete the number [of days] and to ascribe greatness to him; haply you will be thankful.
>
> (2.183–5)

The fast lasts for the thirty days of the month of Ramadan, and consists in abstaining from eating, drinking, smoking and sexual intercourse from before sunrise until after sunset, though these are permissible during the night. The jurists have produced many precise rules based on a further verse:

> It is lawful for you on the night of the fast to go in to your wives; they are a garment for you and you are a garment for them. God knows that you were defrauding yourselves [in this matter], so he has turned to you [in mercy] and forgiven you. So now have intercourse with them, and seek what God has ordained for you [that is, children]. Eat and drink until with dawn you can distinguish a white thread from a black thread. Then observe the fast strictly until night, and do not have intercourse with [your wives], but be assiduous at devotions in the mosques.
>
> (2.187)

v. The Pilgrimage 여즈

The Hajj or pilgrimage proper is sometimes called the Greater Pilgrimage, to distinguish it from the 'Umra or Lesser Pilgrimage. The latter is basically the part of the Greater Pilgrimage which takes place in Mecca itself, but which can be performed in isolation and at any time of the year, as Muhammad and his followers did in the year 629. Every adult Muslim who has the means is required to make the Hajj at least once in his lifetime. The person who has done so may take the appellation of Hajji. Those making the pilgrimage wear two simple white garments, known as the *ihram*, which signify that they are in a state of purity. In Mecca itself they circumambulate the Ka'ba seven times, perform the Salat (with two cycles), and run seven times between two points, Safa and Marwa. This much is the 'Umra. Then, to continue the Hajj, they proceed to Arafat, fifteen miles east of Mecca, where there takes place the station or standing from noon to sunset. On the way back to Mecca there are ceremonies at Muzdalifa and Mina, including what is known as the stoning of the devil, and the sacrifice of an animal. These ceremonies are spread over several days, usually the eighth to the tenth of the month prescribed for the pilgrimage, *Dhu-l-Hijja*.

The Hajj incorporates a number of pagan ceremonies and gives them a monotheistic meaning. In pre-Islamic times, it always took place at the same season of the year, for it was customary to intercalate a month every third year or so to keep the lunar calendar in line with solar seasons. The pilgrimage month and the preceding and following months were regarded as sacred, and in them tribal feuds were in abeyance. After the Hijra, Muhammad himself made the Hajj only once, in 632, shortly before his death, and his example fixed the main details of the Islamic pilgrimage. It was on this occasion that the practice of intercalating a month was abolished by the Qur'an:

> The number of months with God is twelve months, according to his ordinance on the day he created the heavens and the earth; four of these are sacred; that is the sound religion . . . The intercalation [of a month] is an increase of unbelief, by which the unbelievers are misled; they make it lawful in one year and forbid it in [another] year, so that they may make up the number of months which God has made sacred; and thus they make lawful what God has forbidden. (9.36f.)

The Hajj is prescribed for Muslims in two passages: 2.196f. and 22.27f.

vi. The Jihad 非教运功

The Jihad is very occasionally said to be a sixth pillar of Islam. The Arabic word is often translated 'holy war', but it properly means 'striving'. It comes to have the meaning of holy war because in a number of places (e.g. 9.41) the Qur'an commends those who 'strive in the way of God with goods and persons', and this implied fighting. After the Emigrants settled in Medina, they had to face hostile military action from the Meccans, though they may in part have provoked it; and they were encouraged to fight back:

Fight against those who fight against you, but do not trespass [by attacking first].   (2.190)

Those who believed and emigrated and strove in the way of God with goods and persons, and those who took them in and helped them, are [protecting] friends of one another.
                                                        (8.72, 74)

At the time of his great expedition to Tabuk in 631, Muhammad expected all the able-bodied Muslims in Medina to take part; and the Qur'an speaks of those who 'strive in the way of God with goods and persons' as superior to those who do not do so but remain at home (4.95; 9.12f., 24). Thus during Muhammad's lifetime the warlike Jihad against opponents of Islam was a duty, though perhaps not a strict one, and it was largely defensive. It was also stated, however, that if the unbelievers submitted and accepted Islam, fighting was to cease.

After the time of Muhammad, the expeditions undertaken may have been described as 'striving in the way of God', but the purpose was offensive for the most part – namely, to gain booty or to extend the territory under Islamic rule. Conversion of the heathen was not a prominent aim, and in fact most of the opponents were People of the Book, who became protected minorities. In later times, when much of the fighting was done by professional armies, devout Muslims are found saying that actual fighting is only the lesser Jihad, and that the greater Jihad is against the evil in oneself.

4 ISLAMIC LAW

It is roughly correct to say that in Islam the place of theology is taken by law and jurisprudence. Those who deal with the intellectual aspects of the religion are jurists and not theologians, and at the centre of higher education is jurisprudence and not theology. In other words, Islam is more concerned with orthopraxy than orthodoxy. This comes about because the early development of Islam and Christianity took place in very different circumstances. The first Christians lived in the Roman empire, where there was an effective system of law of excellent quality, and for three hundred years the Christians had no political responsibilities. The first Muslims, on the other hand, lived in Mecca, Medina and other parts of Arabia, where nomadic customary law was breaking down because there were now communities based mainly on either commerce or agriculture. From the time of the Hijra the leading Muslims were responsible for the affairs of a political community, and consequently we find in the Qur'an rules for dealing with the practical problems which arose. As the centuries passed these grew into a complete system of law, both public and private, as well as prescriptions for the practice of religion.

This chapter deals exclusively with law in Sunnite Islam. The various Shi'ite groups also had their laws, but formal law was less important for them because their imam had power to overrule previous decisions. Thus there is in Shi'ism no great body of laws and legal thinking comparable to what is found in Sunnism. (See further Noel J. Coulson, *A History of Islamic Law*, pp. 103–19.)

1. THE DEVELOPMENT OF ISLAMIC LAW

Islamic law is known as the Shari'a and covers every aspect of human life – all legal, moral and ritual matters, and even hygiene. To begin with, the Muslims were acting in accordance with traditional Arab custom, but the formation of the politico-religious community at Medina led to new problems which had to be dealt with, and gradually the Qur'an produced a number of rules. These did not deal with all possible problems, however, and in the century after Muhammad they were supplemented by references to his Sunna or standard practice. This was known from thousands of anecdotes about what he had said or done. The most usual word to denote such an anecdote is Hadith, though various others are also used. This was until recently translated as 'tradition' in English, but scholars have come to feel that that term is confusing, and have abandoned it for a transliteration of the Arabic word.

The study of the Shari'a is *fiqh*, 'jurisprudence', and its practitioners are *fuqaha'*, 'jurists'. Another word used is *'ulama'* (anglicized as 'ulama'), which is properly 'those who know' but is mostly translated 'scholars' or 'scholar-jurists'. From shortly after Muhammad's death, pious men used to sit in a mosque and collect around them those interested in discussing the interpretation of the Qur'anic rules and similar matters. Gradually these groups developed into more organized schools, and it was these which produced the *fuqaha'* and *'ulama'*. Eventually four slightly different schools or rites came to be recognized. The alternative term 'rites' indicates that they were not concerned solely with legal theory. Each Muslim had to belong to one of the four rites, and certain matters, such as the disposal of his property at his death, had to be carried out in accordance with the forms of his rite.

Of the four schools thus recognized, that in Medina largely accepted the teaching of one of its leaders, Malik ibn-Anas (d. 796), and its rite came to be known as the Malikite after him. There was an important rival school at Kufa, which was largely shaped by ash-Shaybani (d. 804), but he insisted on giving it the name of his teacher, Abu-Hanifa (d. 767), and so it became known as the Hanafite. The third legal rite is known as the Shafi'ite after ash-Shafi'i (d. 820), who worked in various centres and whose great achievement was the establishing of the new discipline of *usul al-fiqh*, 'the sources or roots of jurisprudence' (of which more will be said presently). The fourth legal rite is the Hanbalite, which takes its name from Ahmad ibn-Hanbal (d. 855), who lived mainly in Baghdad and had a prominent part in the opposition to the Inquisition of al-Ma'mun (as already described). His school also had a distinctive anti-rationalist position in theology. There were some minor schools too, which soon faded out, apart from the Zahirite, which lasted for a century or two.

Because the legal system was largely based on the Sunna of the Prophet, the jurists made much use of Hadiths. In time they realized that it was very easy to invent a Hadith, and they then took steps to ensure that the Hadiths they used were sound. The basic idea was that the text (*matn*) of a Hadith should have a 'support' (*isnad*). This consisted of a list of the persons who had verbally transmitted the text: for example, 'I [the person writing down] was told by A that he had once heard B saying that C reported that Muhammad had said . . .' In this list A, B and C had all to be known to be reliable and trustworthy persons, and for this purpose elaborate biographical dictionaries were built up. If the transmitters were all satisfactory, the Hadith was held to be sound. Collections were made of sound Hadiths, and these came to include several thousands. Six of the collections are regarded as having something like canonical status, and of these the best known and most important are those of al-Bukhari (d. 870) and Muslim (d. 875).

According to ash-Shafi'i's theory of the sources of jurisprudence, there were four of these. The first, obviously, was the Qur'an, and all that was prescribed in it was accepted, provided it had not been abrogated by the Qur'an itself. The second source was the Sunna or practice of the Prophet as known from the sound Hadiths. These two sources, however, did not between them cover all the possible needs of a large community, and so had to be supplemented by two further sources. One of these was *qiyas*, analogy or analogical reasoning; and this meant that some matter for which there was no precise rule was to be treated in accordance with the rule for an analogous matter. Finally some points had to be treated by *ijma'* or consensus. Earlier jurists had thought of this as the consensus of the scholars in, say, Medina, but ash-Shafi'i insisted that it should be the consensus of the whole community of Muslims. For ash-Shafi'i himself, this was a minor source of law, but for later jurists it came to have greater importance, and in a sense everything had to be sanctioned by the consensus of the whole community. The other schools of law accepted ash-Shafi'i's formulations to a great extent, except that the Hanbalites tried to restrict the sources of law to the Qur'an and the Sunna.

A word frequently met with in legal discussions is *ijtihad*. This comes from the same root as Jihad and its basic meaning is 'effort', but it came to have the technical meaning of a qualified jurist's exercise of his independent judgement on a legal matter. This was something which had been done by the founders of the legal schools. In the early tenth century, however, it came to be held that the gates of *ijtihad* had been closed, and this implied that there were to be no further attempts to found a distinctive school. In the nineteenth and twentieth centuries, when many new problems arose, there were discussions about whether the gates of *ijtihad* could be reopened. The conservatives opposed the idea, but the liberals, backed by the pressure of events, insisted on a reopening of the gates, and this in fact came about.

2. SOME PARTICULAR AREAS OF LAW

The total field of Islamic law is vast, but here it will be sufficient to give a general idea of it by looking at some particular areas.

i. Marriage

It is widely known that a Muslim man may have four wives, though it is not so widely known that in the days when there were slaves, he might have as many slave-concubines as he wanted. These facts by themselves, however, give no idea of the great improvements made by Islam in the existing marital practices of the Arabian peninsula. An examination of the records shows that, when Muhammad began to receive revelations, much of the practice was based on matrilineal kinship. This meant that attention was paid only to ancestry on the female side, while ancestry on the male side was neglected and perhaps often unknown. The emphasis on matrilineal kinship, however, did not lead to matriarchy or control by women. There seem to have been large households of people matrilineally related, but the control of such a household would be in the hands of a uterine brother of the senior woman.

Associated with matrilineal kinship was the practice of polyandry, by which a woman had several husbands. These mostly did not live permanently in the woman's household, but were said to 'visit' her, presumably for short periods. Ideally a woman restricted herself to a small number of such partners, but sometimes it may have been difficult not to slip into what was virtually prostitution. There are accounts of how, when a child was born, the mother would assemble her partners, point to one of them and say, 'This is your child'; but this may have happened only after the move from matrilineal to patrilineal kinship had begun.

One of the features of seventh-century Arabia was the breakdown of tribalism and the growth of individualism. This was the case in Mecca above all, where it had been fostered by the growth of commerce. It has already been noted how the great merchants would form partnerships with members of clans other than their own. Such persons would also be anxious that the wealth they had gathered would on their death be inherited by their own sons rather than their sisters' sons.

The new religion of Islam supported the idea that a woman should have sexual relations with only one man at a time. There does not seem to be any verse in the Qur'an prescribing this, but the Qur'an insists that a woman who has been divorced (presumably from her one husband) should observe a waiting period of three monthly courses before remarrying (2.226–8). This would ensure that the paternity of any child was certain.

Another change made under Islam was that the matrilineal household was replaced by what is called a virilocal one – that is, one consisting of a man, his wife or wives and his descendants. Muhammad gave the example of this. He had his house in Medina, and as he acquired wives, each had her apartment round the courtyard. Probably some of the other Muslim men, especially those from Mecca, had their own houses. This is the background against which the chief verse about marriage is to be understood: 'If you fear that you may not deal equitably with the orphans, marry such women as seem good to you, twos and threes and fours; and if you fear that you may not be fair [to several wives], then one only or what your right hand possesses [slaves]' (4.3).

This verse is thought to have been revealed shortly after the battle of Uhud, in which over seventy Muslims had been killed. The rule that a Muslim may not have more than four wives was derived from it by jurists, but the verse itself is not placing a restriction on a hitherto larger number of wives, but is encouraging men to take more wives; and this would ensure that the widows of those killed would be cared for by Muslim men and would not revert to polyandry. We do not know what proportion of these women had been restricting themselves to one partner, but presumably it was high.

In a place such as Medina, where polyandry was a long-established accepted custom, it could not be eradicated all at once. There are many verses in the Qur'an which seem to be dealing with this problem, but their interpretation is sometimes difficult, and the later commentators, who had no idea of the actual situation with which the Qur'an was dealing, do not help. One important verse is 4.24. It begins by saying that men may not marry *muhsanat* (or *muhsinat*), and this word is usually translated 'married women' or 'chaste women', but it presumably had the precise meaning of women restricting themselves to one partner. Later in the verse, Muslim men are told that they may have other women as wives, but that they themselves must be *muhsinin*, not *musafihin*. These words are translated as 'in chaste wedlock, not debauchery'; while they are masculine in form, they presumably mean both that the men are not to have relations with polyandric women and also that the women are to restrict themselves to one partner. The implication seems to be that polyandry was still being practised to some extent, and the Arabic words translated 'marry' and 'marriage' can apply to such unions. The point seems to be confirmed by another verse: 'Base women to base men and base men to base women; and good women to good men and good men to good women' (24.26). The word 'base' here presumably means those practising polyandry, and they are thus placed in a kind of ghetto and cut off from the rest of the community. There was thus strong pressure against polyandry, and it seems to have died out within a generation or so.

These are the main points regarding the reform of marital practice by the Qur'an. Various other matters are also dealt with, such as the forbidden degrees (close relatives one is not allowed to marry) and the dowry or bride-wealth.

ii. Security of life

In respect of security of life the Qur'an did not introduce anything new, but reinforced the existing system so as to exclude various shortcomings. The existing system was based on retaliation, or the *lex talionis*, which is expressed in the Biblical phrase 'life shall go for life, eye for eye, tooth for tooth . . .' (Deuteronomy 19.21). To the modern person, this may seem a barbaric practice, but it is in fact an effective way of maintaining a high degree of security of life in early forms of society where there is no strong central authority capable of establishing a police force. As practised in pre-Islamic Arabia, it meant that when someone was killed, it was a duty for his next of kin or some other member of the killer's social group to kill either the killer himself or a member of his social group. There is here the underlying idea of communal responsibility, and this leads to the family or clan or tribe discouraging its members from taking a life in case that leads to reprisals and the creating of a blood feud. Mosaic law accepted this general idea, but aimed at preventing retaliation for accidental killing by establishing cities of refuge.

The system as practised in Arabia worked up to a point, but it sometimes broke down. There is a well-known case where a great chief was killed, but his tribe, after killing a young man from the other tribe, claimed that this was not enough and was only the equivalent of the chief's shoe-latchet. The result was a war that went on for years. Another weak point was that after a life had been taken for a life, the relatives of the second victim might want to avenge him, especially where he was not the original killer.

One of the points made by Islam was to regard the community of believers as a single great tribe; and for this reason a person who killed another Muslim wrongfully was to be rejected by the whole community. An article in the Constitution of Medina stated that when a believer is killed (by another believer) 'the believers are against [the murderer] entirely, and nothing is permissible to them except to oppose him' (§ 21; cf. § 13; see also my *Muhammad at Medina*, p. 266). Within the Islamic community, however, it had to be recognized that there continued to exist smaller social groupings which could be hostile to one another. The Qur'an therefore makes provision for retaliation between Muslims.

> O you who believe, retaliation for one killed is prescribed
> for you, the free man [to die] for the free man, the slave
> for the slave, the woman for the woman; and [the
> offender] who is forgiven [for his offence] by his brother
> should respond as is customary and make payment
> amicably; this is an alleviation and a mercy from your Lord.
> (2.178; cf. 5.45; 16.126; 42.40)

This is a complex verse, and some parts are difficult to translate, but certain points seem to be clear. It is in part an encouragement to Muslims to accept blood-money instead of an actual life when someone is killed. During Muhammad's lifetime, the blood-wit for an adult male seems to have been raised to a hundred camels or the equivalent in money; this is a considerable sum and might encourage the victim's group not to insist on blood. Conservatives and traditionalists, however, taunted those who accepted a blood-wit with being content with milk instead of blood. Several of the verses dealing with retaliation insist that it should not be more than the action to be avenged, and one verse (17.33) warns against going to excess.

The Qur'an also makes provision for cases of accidental killing: 'It is not for a believer to kill a believer unless by mistake; he who kills a believer by mistake [must] set free a believing slave and pay blood-money to [the victim's] family' (4.94). There are slight variations if the believer belongs to a group hostile to the Islamic community or only in alliance with it. The freeing of a believing slave was perhaps intended to preserve the number of believing freemen.

The final words of the verse quoted above (2.178) are: 'as for him who after that provokes hostility, for him is a painful punishment'. The word translated 'provokes hostility' is not altogether clear, but it probably means taking retaliation for what was itself an act of retaliation; and this was something which had happened in pre-Islamic times. Whatever the precise meaning of this verse, it is certain that Muhammad stopped any such action and insisted that, when vengeance had been taken which was not greater than the crime, peace had been restored between the two groups involved; and he had sufficient authority to enforce the principle. The substitution of blood-money would, of course, lessen the danger of a continuing feud.

Slight as the changes in this field made by the Qur'an and Muhammad may seem, they produced a system of social security for the embryonic Islamic state which enabled it to expand into an empire.

There was an attempt to make property safer by ordering that a thief, male or female, should have his or her hand cut off (5.38). This rather severe punishment has to be linked with the idea of the communal responsibility of the group. In so far as the thief could no longer work effectively, the group would have to maintain him. In a modern society, however, this means imposing a burden on the community as a whole.

iii. Inheritance

The problem facing early Islam in respect of inheritance was brought about by the transition to individualism from communalism, especially the matrilineal communalism of Medina. In that society, strange as it may seem, a woman could own no property that she herself could administer; it had to be administered for her by a male relative on the female side. Probably most of the property was held in common by the matrilineal household. As individualism developed, both in Medina and in the more patrilineal society of Mecca, what happened was that powerful individuals seized much more than their fair share of the property. This is the situation with which the Qur'an tried to deal.

After outlining fair treatment for orphans, there is a long passage giving precise rules for inheritance. The first section may be usefully quoted:

> God charges you in respect of your children [to leave] to the male the equivalent of the share of two females; if there are more than two females, they have two-thirds of what [their father] left, and if there is one, she has the half; to [a man's] parents, to each of them, [is to be given] a sixth of what he left, if he has a son; but if he has no son, and his parents are his heirs, then to his mother is given the third; but if he has brothers, then to his mother is given a sixth, after any bequest he made and any debt has been paid.   (4.11)

The passage then goes on to give rules for a number of other contingencies, including the division of the property of deceased wives. Later jurists had a wonderful time working out how precisely the rules were to be applied in various likely and unlikely sets of circumstances. In Muhammad's time these rules certainly led to a fairer distribution of the wealth of the community. The right of a woman to hold property was recognized, but in most cases, though not in all, her share was only half a man's.

iv. Food laws

After moving to Medina the Muslims became aware that the Jews observed certain laws about food; and, probably because they were still hoping that the Jews would accept Muhammad as a prophet, a verse was revealed to the effect that Jewish food was allowable for them, and their food allowable for Jews (5.3). They may have found Jewish restrictions irksome, however, when they understood them more fully, and another verse speaks of restrictions being imposed on the Jews as a punishment for wrongdoing on their part (4.169). Another verse (5.5), presumably later still, gives a detailed statement of what is forbidden for Muslims – namely, carrion, blood, pork, what has been dedicated to a pagan god, what has been strangled or felled or gored or died by falling from a height; what has been mangled by wild animals is forbidden unless the victim is found alive and put to death in the proper fashion. The proper method of killing is not explicitly stated in the Qur'an, but it consists in cutting the throat and allowing the blood to drain out.

Islam also forbids the drinking of any alcoholic beverage. This is based on Qur'anic verses, especially 5.90, which strictly forbids the drinking of *khamr*. This is properly the fermented juice of the grape, but by the principle of analogy it was eventually understood to include anything alcoholic. In an earlier verse (2.219) the prohibition of wine is not absolute, and there was also said to be something good in wine. Wine is mentioned as one of the delights of Paradise. There are some reports about drunkenness among Muhammad's Companions, and this was doubtless a large part of the reason for the prohibition, but there may have been some others, such as the fact that wine was imported from hostile countries, or perhaps had some connection with pagan rites.

v. Usury

The prohibition of usury is somehow mixed up with Muhammad's relations with the Jews of Medina. For a long time he regarded them as fellow believers, but when he appealed to them as to the Muslims for contributions, they seem to have said that they would give only a loan for which they would receive interest. One aspect of the wrongdoing of the Jews, for which they were punished by food restrictions, was 'their taking usury, when they had been forbidden to do so' (4.160); and this presumably was taken as meaning that the Jews should have accepted the Muslims as fellow believers and not demanded interest. The Qur'an also warned Muslims against taking usury and suggested that those who did so were in danger of hell (2.275–81; 3.130; 30.39f.). In modern times this has been understood as any interest on loans; but under Muhammad and in early Islam we may be certain that it was not applied in any way that impeded the normal mercantile activity of Mecca.

vi. Slavery

Early Islam accepted slavery as it was then practised in Arabia. Often slaves were members of other tribes who had been captured in fighting and then sold to remote tribes, from whom they had little chance of escaping. Captured women and children could also be sold, and male slaves had often been slaves since childhood. After the Jewish clan of Qurayza surrendered to the Muslims (as mentioned earlier) the women and children were sold as slaves. The Qur'an (4.36) insists that slaves are to be treated kindly; and the freeing of a slave, especially a Muslim slave, was seen as a pious act (24.33); Abu-Bakr was said to have bought and freed several slaves before the Hijra. Slaves could own property; and this meant that in some cases they could earn money with which to buy freedom.

vii. The control and administration of affairs

The Qur'an says hardly anything about the control of the affairs of the Islamic state. In the Constitution of Medina, Muhammad was one clan chief among nine, though he was also accepted as the prophet and it was stipulated that disputes were to be referred to him for settlement. The Qur'an (8.1, 41) states that a fifth of the booty taken in raids was to be paid to him. With his successes against the Meccans, his power gradually increased, and in his last years there was little opposition to his decisions. Much of this autocratic power was inherited by the caliphs with the consensus of the community. By Arab custom, the chief usually consulted with the leading men of his tribe, and there seems to have been a little of this in the caliphate. Apart from this, however, Muslim rulers through the centuries have tended to practise a form of autocracy, although because there are no precise Qur'anic rulings, some modern Islamic states have managed to establish a form of democracy. When it comes to parliamentary legislation, conservative jurists claim a right to decide whether new laws are in accordance with the Shari'a, but the statesmen are unwilling to concede this.

5 ISLAMIC THEOLOGY

Although theology was subordinate to jurisprudence according to the usual Muslim outlook, in time there came to be a large body of scholars who gave much thought to the exposition of the intellectual aspect of Islamic belief – that is, to theology. The development of theology in Islam, however, was rather different from that in Christianity, because from the first Islam was a political as well as a religious community. The consequence of this was that the earliest theological arguments normally had political implications. As has already been noted, the question of whether the Qur'an was created or uncreated was basically a political dispute.

1. THE EARLY SECTS

The first appearance of sectarianism is usually taken to be in 656 in an army in Iraq led by the caliph 'Ali. This army had just defeated the forces of the Meccan group opposed to 'Ali's assumption of the caliphate and was preparing to march against his rival, Mu'awiya. A considerable body of men seceded or went out (*kharaju*) from the army because they disapproved of some decisions 'Ali had taken. These are regarded as the first of the sect of the Kharijites or Khawarij (the singular is Khariji), which proliferated during the Umayyad period and had many subdivisions. 'Ali met some of the grievances of the first group and they returned to his army; but shortly afterwards a second group with similar grievances 'went out', refused to be reconciled and were eventually massacred. This shows a division within 'Ali's army between those who criticized him and those who wholeheartedly supported him; and there were doubtless others with less definite views. Let us look first at the supporters of 'Ali.

Those who gave wholehearted support to 'Ali seem to have been in the habit of referring to themselves as 'the Party' or Shi'a, and this became the name of the sect as it developed a more definite character, and gives us the adjective Shi'ite. From an early date there seem to have been people who thought that 'Ali should have been Muhammad's immediate successor. Those who adopted such views may have wanted above all a charismatic leader. The change from the previous nomadic life in the Arabian deserts to membership of the Muslim armies and life in camp cities must have been very upsetting. A significant proportion of those who became Shi'ites were from southern Arab tribes, and in the south of Arabia there had been for centuries a tradition of semi-divine kings. This may have unconsciously led them to seek a charismatic leader with more than human powers. It would also be natural to look for this leader in Muhammad's clan, since there was a strong Arab belief that desirable qualities were genetically handed down in certain clans.

After 'Ali's death al-Hasan, a son by Muhammad's daughter Fatima, was easily induced to come to terms with Mu'awiya, who now assumed the caliphate and founded the Umayyad dynasty. His full brother al-Husayn, however, tried to claim the caliphate after the death of Mu'awiya, but he received little support and with a small band of followers was massacred at Kerbela in Iraq – an event still annually commemorated by the Shi'ites. In 685, while Ibn az-Zubayr, leading a rebellion against the Umayyads, was in control of Arabia and Iraq, a man called al-Mukhtar organized a Shi'ite rising in Kufa, ostensibly on behalf of Muhammad ibn al-Hanafiyya, a son of 'Ali though not by Fatima; but after two years the Shi'ites were overpowered. An important point is that al-Mukhtar was strongly supported by 'clients' or *mawali* – that is, non-Arab Muslims from the Aramaean and Persianized inhabitants of Iraq and the surrounding regions. The clients felt at a disadvantage compared with the Arab Muslims, and from this time onwards seem to have looked to the Shi'ites for an improvement in their position. The 'Abbasid armies which brought about the downfall of the Umayyads had large numbers of clients, perhaps a majority, and the chief general was a client.

After al-Mukhtar's defeat, the Shi'ites remained quiescent until the last decade or so of Umayyad rule, when there were one or two small revolts. The most significant was one led by Zayd, a great-great-grandson of Muhammad. This was the origin of the Zaydite form of Shi'ism, according to which any member of Muhammad's clan of Hashim may become imam (as the Shi'ites call the leader of the community), provided he makes the claim openly and maintains it by force. Although Zayd's rising was soon put down, there were later some small groups which claimed to follow him and which for a time maintained small autonomous states. The most noteworthy were the Zaydite imams of San'a (in the Yemen), who continued to exist into the present century. In contrast to other Shi'ites, the Zaydites allowed that Abu-Bakr and 'Umar were rightful rulers, while holding that 'Ali should have succeeded Muhammad.

The rising which brought the 'Abbasids to power gained some Shi'ite support by claiming that the imamate had passed from Muhammad ibn-al-Hanafiyya to his son Abu-Hashim, who had then transferred it to their family. About the time of the caliph Harun ar-Rashid, however, they officially abandoned this claim and instead maintained that the rightful imam after the Prophet had been their ancestor, his uncle al-'Abbas. Under the Umayyads, the Islamic state continued to be thought of as a federation of Arab tribes, but after the coming to power of the 'Abbasids, with their support from clients, this conception soon disappeared.

The early 'Abbasid caliphs themselves seem to have favoured Shi'ite ideas to the extent that these suggested that the caliph or imam had autocratic powers. As was seen in Chapter 2, this led to the so-called Inquisition inaugurated by al-Ma'mun. The basic point was that, if the Qur'an is created, then it is not eternal and can be altered by a divinely inspired imam. The abandonment about 850 of the policy of the Inquisition was tantamount to an admission that the caliph was not divinely inspired, and it also meant that the Islamic state became officially Sunnite.

Shi'ite sources speak of a continuing body of people who acknowledged a series of imams in succession to al-Husayn, each the son of the previous one. The fourth, fifth and sixth were 'Ali Zayn-al-Abidin (d. c.714), Muhammad al-Baqir (d. 733) and Ja'far as-Sadiq (d. 765). These men, though acknowledged as imams by some people, seem to have been completely quiescent, since otherwise they would have been imprisoned or executed by the Umayyad or 'Abbasid caliphs. Up to this point the Shi'ite movement seems to have been rather formless and to have comprised people with varying views.

After the death of Ja'far in 765 a split occurred. A group who wanted a less quiescent imam maintained that Ja'far had nominated as his successor his son Isma'il. Isma'il probably predeceased Ja'far, but some of this group denied the fact. Those who accepted it held that Isma'il's son Muhammad had become the next imam. Working largely in concealment, they gradually built up a strong body and in 909 they were able to wrest control of Tunisia (or Ifriqiyya) from the governing dynasty. The leaders of this body, who were recognized as the true imams in succession to Ja'far, are known as the Fatimid dynasty. In 969 they conquered Egypt, founded the city of Cairo as their base and maintained their rule there until 1171. After their expulsion from Egypt, groups continued to exist in parts of Arabia and Iran, but at the time of the great Mongol invasion in the thirteenth century, most moved to India, where there was a complex history of division and reunion. The main group at the present time are the followers of the Aga Khan, who is regarded as the true imam in unbroken succession. This sect as a whole is known as the Isma'ilites or Isma'iliyya; but sometimes they are referred to as the Seveners or Sab'iyya, because they broke off from the other Shi'ites at the time of the seventh imam.

Those Shi'ites who did not follow Isma'il held that the true imam after Ja'far was another son, Musa (d. 799), and he was followed by his son 'Ali ar-Rida (d. 818). The caliph al-Ma'mun tried to get the support of the Shi'ite movement by naming 'Ali ar-Rida as his successor, but the latter died prematurely in mysterious circumstances, and al-Ma'mun abandoned the implied policy. After this the general Shi'ite movement seems gradually to have taken a more definite form, and the 'Abbasid caliphs came to have suspicions of those regarded as true imams; but did not go further than imprisonment, although some Shi'ites claim that all the later imams were executed by the 'Abbasids. The eleventh imam, al-Hassan al-'Askari, died on or about 1 January 874 and was succeeded by his son Muhammad al-Qa'im. What exactly happened next is not clear, but the Shi'ite leaders claimed that he had gone into occultation. By this they meant that he was inaccessible to ordinary Muslims, though he still had a *wakil* or agent with whom he was in touch, and this person was named.

On the death of the fourth Wakil in about 940, however, no other was appointed, and this was considered to be the beginning of the greater occultation. This continues to the present day, for it is held that the Twelfth Imam's life has been miraculously prolonged, and that he will return at an appropriate time to set everything right in the world.

This subject of Shi'ites is best known as the Imamites, but it is sometimes called the Twelvers or Ithna 'Ashariyya because of its doctrine of twelve imams. It is often referred to simply as the Shi'ites, since it is the largest subsect. For the historian the doctrine of the occultation can be seen as a subtle move by some of the leading members of the sect to avoid various difficulties. Several of the recognized imams had had little understanding of public affairs. By saying that the imam was in occultation, control of the group passed into the hands of those who had some such understanding and who wanted to remain at peace with the 'Abbasid caliphate. Some of them seem to have been involved in the financial affairs of the caliphate but to have wanted to keep aloof from its actual policies. The new doctrine enabled them to work with the government, while partly staying apart from it. From this point, the Imamites were at peace with the caliphs, and no change occurred until the establishment of Safavid rule in Iran at the beginning of the sixteenth century.

At the present time the Imamites are much more numerous than the Zaydites and Isma'ilites, but the three groups together form only one tenth of the total number of Muslims.

In 'Ali's army in 656, besides the forerunners of the later Shi'ites, there were those who 'went out' from him and so became the first Kharijites. One of their basic ideas was that if a Muslim committed a grave sin, this excluded him from the community of Muslims. The underlying thought was that the community of Muslims were the people of Paradise, whereas the grave sinner was destined for hell and association with him would endanger the future of those destined for Paradise. This body may not have had links with the group which assassinated 'Uthman, but they thought the act was justified, because 'Uthman, in not punishing a man who had committed a grave sin, himself committed a grave sin. They further thought that 'Ali had not been sufficiently sympathetic to those who killed 'Uthman. It was not only 'Ali, however, who attracted their anger, for while seven small Kharijite risings are reported during his caliphate, there were about twenty during that of Mu'awiya.

As already suggested, the Kharijite movement as a whole is to be seen as a reaction to the sense of insecurity and crisis brought about by the transition from nomadic life in the desert to life in the Muslim armies. While those who became Shi'ites thought they gained security from a charismatic leader, the Kharijites looked for security in membership of a charismatic tribe. The Islamic Umma as a whole was such a community, and they wanted to preserve its special character. This feeling probably linked up with pre-Islamic attitudes to the tribe or clan, since traditionally what made life meaningful was belonging to a tribe or clan with high qualities. We are told that in the risings against 'Ali and Mu'awiya the numbers involved varied from thirty to five hundred, with an average of about two hundred, so that when these insurgents went into the desert they formed something like a small nomadic tribe.

During the civil war from 684 to 692, two subsects of Kharijites appeared, stimulating theological thinking. The first were the Azariqa or Azraqites. When Ibn az-Zubayr occupied Basra, they retired into the mountains eastwards and maintained themselves for a decade or more, sometimes threatening Basra. They held that they alone were the true Islamic community, that the existing authorities had sinned and that anyone who did not abandon the existing authorities and join them in their camp had also sinned and should be put to death. On the basis of this theory they became terrorists, engaging in widespread massacres.

The other subsect were the Najdites (Najadat or Najdiyya), who established themselves in central Arabia and for a time controlled a large part of the country. Originally they thought like the Azraqites, but it soon became clear that they could not kill or banish from their territory everyone who committed a single act of theft or other crime. To justify their lesser punishments for such people, they distinguished between fundamentals and non-fundamentals, and they further held that a single wrong act was a non-fundamental, whereas persistence in sin and wrongdoing was idolatry, which was a fundamental. They allowed that God might punish single acts of wrongdoing by committing a person to hell, but this would be for a limited period, and the person would eventually enter Paradise.

While the Najdites were concerned with the problems of a large community under autonomous Kharijite rule, there were in Basra many moderate Kharijites whose problem was how to live under non-Kharijite rule. Some held they were in 'the sphere of prudent fear' (dar at-taqiyya), where it was permissible to conceal their true views. At first they tended to say that the non-Kharijite authorities were unbelievers or idolaters, but gradually they came to see that this name was inappropriate for God-fearing Muslims who differed from themselves on a few points, and instead they called them monotheists (muwahhidun). They also discussed many other theological questions. Indeed, in the period from about 690 to 730 Basra was the scene of theological debates which largely determined the future course of Islamic theology.

Perhaps the most positive contribution of the Kharijites to the Islamic community as a whole was their insistence on the

Qur'an as the primary source of law and belief. Some of the earliest Kharijites had formulated this in the words 'no decision but God's' (*la hukm illa li-llah*) or 'the decision is God's alone'; and by this they meant that public decisions must be based on principles taken from the Qur'an and not on traditional Arab custom. As was seen in the last chapter, this became the basis of Islamic law, though supplemented by the divinely inspired Sunna of Muhammad.

One small group of quiescent Kharijites in Basra is known as the Waqifites or Waqifa, because they suspended judgement (*waqafu*) about certain questions. They held that one could not know the ultimate fate of a wrongdoer – that is, whether he belonged to the people of Paradise or the people of hell – but that in the meantime he should continue to be regarded as a member of the Islamic community. This group is not important in itself, but it shows a movement away from Kharijism towards another group of sects known as the Murji'ites or Murji'a.

Much of our knowledge of these early sects comes from various later writers, sometimes called heresiographers. The most important books are *Maqalat al-islamiyyin* by al-Ash'ari (d. 935), *Al-Farq bayn al-firaq* by al-Baghdadi (d. 1037) and *Kitab al-milal wa-n-nihal* by ash-Shahrastani (d. 1153). These writers tended to accept the labels given to groups in the material they consulted without paying close attention to the person attaching the label. As a result we find that ash-Shahrastani, when he comes to speak of the Murji'ites, has to distinguish between Murji'a of the Kharijites, those of the Qadarites, those of the Jabrites and pure Murji'a; and finally he has to speak of Abu-Hanifa (after whom the Hanafite legal school is named) as a Murji'ite of the Sunna, because such a person, though called a Murji'ite by opponents, could not be regarded as a heretic. This shows that there was no closely knit sect of Murji'ites, but that the name designated a trend of thought found among people whose other views differed widely.

The name is derived from the participle *murji*, 'one postponing'. The term seems to have been first applied to those who postponed a decision about who was right and who was wrong in the fighting which followed the death of 'Uthman in 656. Perhaps these persons should be seen as trying to heal the rift that was opening at that time between various groups. Later the term was understood more generally as the postponement of a decision about the grave sinner, and this implied accepting him as a member of the community. It was said to be derived from the words 'some are postponed for the command of God' (9.106). Though the term 'postponement' was not used in later Sunnism, its political implications were accepted.

The Umayyads defended the legitimacy of their caliphate in various ways. One was to say that Mu'awiya was the avenger of blood for 'Uthman in accordance with traditional Arab ideas. Latterly, however, they came to place more emphasis on the claim that their rule had been determined by God, and this claim they justified by verses from the Qur'an. They also held that their acts were in accordance with God's determination. Some of the opponents of the Umayyads countered these arguments by what amounted to a doctrine of human free will. These people were called Qadarites. They seem to have been more of a sect than the Murji'ites, but there were different groups among them. Some of the Kharijite rebels in the closing years of the Umayyad dynasty are said to have held Qadarite views.

The Jabrites (Jabriyya, Mujbira) were probably not a sect in any real sense. Rather 'Jabrite' was a term of abuse used by Qadarites and others for those of more predestinarian views. It would apply to many of the main central body of Muslims. While there is thus much information about the heretical sects of the Umayyad and early 'Abbasid periods, it should be emphasized that there was also what might be called a general religious movement – that is, a body of pious Muslims who held the essentials of what was later considered to be true Islam. These might be called 'orthodox', but, as already indicated, this term is not appropriate in Islam, and it is preferable to speak of the general religious movement or of mainstream Islam.

What is meant by these terms is roughly what is now called Sunnism, but the conception of Sunnism took shape only gradually. To begin with, the various groups in mainstream Islam were more aware of their differences than of what they had in common. Some called themselves by such names as 'the people of the Sunna' (Ahl as-Sunna) or 'the people of the Sunna and the Community' (Ahl as-Sunna wa-l-Jama'a), but these terms, as originally used, might exclude some who would now be regarded as Sunnites. The adjective Sunni (Sunnite) does not seem to be recorded until near the end of the tenth century, and this is perhaps the time when the Sunnites became aware of what they had in common.

2. THE DEVELOPMENT OF SUNNITE THEOLOGY

While the early theological discussions centred round the religio-political problems of the Islamic state, a fresh element entered in the early ninth century. This was the Hellenistic culture dominant in the new provinces of Iraq, Syria and Egypt. In Iraq there were Christian colleges teaching Greek medicine, science and philosophy in the local language. To begin with, the Muslims were probably chiefly interested in the medicine, but the caliph al-Ma'mun established an institute, the Bayt al-Hikma, for the translation of large numbers of Greek books, and this institute did not confine itself to medicine. At the same time, a number of persons educated in these Hellenistic schools became Muslims.

In the theological field some Muslim thinkers came to realize that Greek methods of argument were a useful weapon, against both Muslim opponents and non-Muslims. One of the first to do so was Dirar ibn-'Amr, about whom much more has been discovered recently. He was active in Basra in the last decade of the eighth century and led theological discussions in which some use was made of Greek ideas. In this matter he was the forerunner of an important group or sect known as the Mu'tazila or Mu'tazilites. They accepted the belief in human free will and so were sometimes called Qadarites, although the anti-govern-ment attitude of the original Qadarites had ceased to be meaningful after the fall of the Umayyads. For a time the Mu'tazilites were in close association with the 'Abbasid caliphs, and it was they who provided the theological arguments for the createdness of the Qur'an and so supported al-Ma'mun's policy of the Inquisition.

The Mu'tazilites sometimes called themselves 'the people of unity and justice' (Ahl at-tawhid wa-l-'adl). The unity was that of God. They insisted that divine attributes such as knowledge (or omniscience) had no existence of any sort except in God's essence. It followed that the Qur'an, if it was uncreated, was some sort of eternal existent besides God's essence, and so an infringement of his unity; and for this reason they insisted that it was created. There were, of course, various other subtle arguments on both sides. While the Mu'tazilites may have inherited from the Kharijites a concern that people should fully obey God's laws, the principle of justice which they highlighted was God's justice; and they made the point that God could not justly condemn human beings to hell unless they were responsible for their acts. This was thus an argument for human free will.

Three other principles were also used to give a precise definition of Mu'tazilism. One amounted to belief in Paradise and hell. Another was that the grave sinner was neither a believer nor an unbeliever but was in an intermediate position. Finally they held that it was the duty of all Muslims to maintain justice in the public sphere and to oppose injustice in whatever way was open to them, whether by word, action or force of arms. This is known as 'commending the right and forbidding the wrong' (al-amr bi-l-ma'ruf wa-n-nahy 'an al-munkar).

After the abandonment of the policy of the Inquisition in about 850 the Mu'tazilites lost their political importance and became a body of somewhat academic theologians, with schools in both Basra and Baghdad. An important new development in Islamic theology is associated with the school in Basra. A man called al-Ash'ari (873–935) studied for some years there, occasionally giving lectures, and might possibly have become the next head of the school. About 912, however, he decided to abandon Mu'tazilism and to adopt the more conservative form of dogmatic belief professed by the theological Hanbalites. At the same time, he began to defend these beliefs by the methods of argument he had learned as a Mu'tazilite, thus inaugurating the new discipline of Kalam or philosophical theology in Sunnite Islam. This discipline soon had large numbers of exponents, and by the eleventh century Ash'arite Kalam could be considered the main form of Islamic theology. It dominated the central Islamic lands for centuries.

This is the common account of the origin of Kalam, but it may exaggerate the contribution of al-Ash'ari himself. Other scholars had been working along similar lines, and at the time of his conversion to conservative beliefs there was already in existence a group to which he attached himself. Slight differences between al-Ash'ari and some of these others were later discussed by one of his pupils. Much here is obscure, but it is clear that by the middle of the eleventh century the main practitioners of Kalam thought of themselves as Ash'arites. It is often also stated that there was a parallel school of philosophical theology in Samarkand founded by al-Maturidi (d. 944). This school certainly existed and flourished locally, but it had little influence on other parts of the Islamic world. The suggestion that it was on a level with that of the Ash'arites comes from an Ottoman writer in the sixteenth century; and he exalted its position because it was associated with the Hanafite legal school and the Ottoman empire was officially Hanafite.

A difference between the Ash'arites and Hanbalites on the one hand and the Maturidites and Hanafites on the other is that the former held that faith could increase and decrease whereas the latter maintained that it could not. The underlying idea of the first is that many good works show greater faith and bad acts imply bad faith. The basis of the other view is that faith makes people believers, and they are either believers or unbelievers, there being no half-way house.

The whole discipline of Kalam or philosophical theology was strenuously opposed by the theologians of the Hanbalite legal school. Although al-Ash'ari had adopted their position in dogmatic matters, they would have nothing to do with his methods of argument. The Hanbalite type of theology has continued alongside Kalam, because in Islam there is no official body comparable to the Christian ecumenical councils which can give a definite statement about what constitutes true Islamic belief.

Numerous writings by members of the Ash'arite school during the tenth and eleventh centuries have been preserved, and something is known about the writers, but here it will be sufficient to speak about the man who was chiefly responsible for a step forward in the development of Kalam. This was Abu-

Hamid Muhammad al-Ghazali (1058–1111). He was born and brought up in eastern Iran, and studied jurisprudence and theology in the recently founded Nizamiyya college in Nishapur. His outstanding intellectual qualities were soon evident and appreciated. At the early age of thirty-three he was appointed to the prestigious position of professor and director of the Nizamiyya college in Baghdad, where his primary duty was to teach jurisprudence. He had become aware of the threat to theology from the Arabic philosophers (as will be explained more fully in the next section), and in Baghdad he set himself to master the writings of Avicenna and other philosophers and to write a refutation of such views as he considered false. In doing this, however, he came to appreciate the possible use of a discipline such as Aristotelian logic; and when he realized that nothing in this logic was contrary to basic Islamic belief, he set about writing books encouraging his fellow theologians to employ it more fully. This many of them did.

After four years in Baghdad al-Ghazali went through a spiritual crisis, retired from his professorship and entered into a kind of monastic life in accordance with the Islamic tradition of Sufism. He made the pilgrimage to Mecca in the closing months of 1096, but his movements after that are not altogether clear. By about 1100, however, he had established a hostel in his native town of Tus, where young men came to join him in living the Sufi life. About 1105 he was prevailed upon to return to teaching in the Nizamiyya college in Nishapur. He continued there for at least three years, but then, presumably because of ill-health, retired to Tus, where he died in December 1111.

Al-Ghazali left a large number of writings, and others have been falsely attributed to him. The genuine ones include a vast work on the revival of the religious sciences, which has forty chapters or sections, each of which forms a small volume in translation. This work gives a full account of his understanding of Islam after his 'conversion'. So far as his contemporaries and successors were concerned, he was primarily a jurist, and he wrote some important works on jurisprudence. The work which has had most influence in the West, however, is a kind of spiritual autobiography, *The Deliverer from Error (al-Munqidh min ad-dalal)*. In this he describes his search for truth after going through a period of scepticism; but he gives the account in what seems to be a logical rather than a chronological order.

The initial area he approached in his search was the discipline of Kalam, with which, of course, he was involved for many years, first in studying and then in teaching; but latterly he came to feel that there were ultimate questions to which it could give no answer. The next area of search was philosophy, where again he was disappointed. Third, he looked at a form of the Isma'ilite heresy which was making anti-'Abbasid propaganda in the caliphate; but he seems to have studied this less because he was attracted by its doctrines than because the caliph had asked him to write a refutation. Fourth came the Islamic Sufi or mystical tradition; and this led him to the conclusion that he had proceeded as far as was possible by rational methods and that what he now needed was to gain direct experience of ultimate things by living the life of a Sufi. This conclusion, accompanied by a kind of physical breakdown, led to his retirement from teaching.

This is the kind of personal statement that makes a powerful appeal to the Western mind. The book became known in Europe about the middle of the nineteenth century, and because of its attractiveness European scholars then devoted much more attention to other works of al-Ghazali than to comparable works of other Muslim scholars.

3. THE ARABIC PHILOSOPHERS

While groups of theologians were making use of Greek ideas to a limited extent, there were a few Muslim thinkers who accepted Greek philosophy in a wholehearted way. One of the earliest was a man of Arab descent, al-Kindi (d. 870). Of more importance were al-Farabi (d. 950) and Ibn-Sina (or Avicenna in Latin) (d. 1037). Through his writings al-Kindi did much to spread the knowledge of Greek thought and to bring it into line with Islamic beliefs, at least of a Mu'tazilite type; in particular, he changed the Greek conception of the emanation of the world from God into one of its creation by him out of nothing. Al-Farabi and Avicenna produced a virtually complete philosophy which was basically a form of Neoplatonism; but they were careful to express it in a way that was compatible with the Islamic conception of God. They did not include many other points of Islamic belief, however, and were regarded as heretics by the theologians. The latter, for their part, mostly did not bother to read the works of the philosophers, and possibly in many cases could not understand them; but there were many well-educated Muslims who were turning to the philosophers rather than the theologians. This caused concern to a few theologians, and around 1090 al-Ghazali (as already mentioned in the previous section) procured copies of the works of al-Farabi and Avicenna, and by his private reading mastered them; it would have been difficult for one in his position to go to a philosopher for instruction.

After his study of the philosophers, al-Ghazali wrote an exposition of their beliefs, primarily those of Avicenna, and then went on to write a refutation of them. His exposition is in some ways clearer than the writings of Avicenna himself. In his refutation he called attention to twenty errors of the philosophers, of which the most serious were that they held the world had existed from eternity, and so had not been created; that God knew only universals and not particulars; and that resurrection was of the soul only, not of the body.

Al-Ghazali called his book *The Incoherence of the Philosophers*, because it showed that their arguments were not as watertight as they claimed. In the latter half of the twelfth century there appeared in the Islamic West a refutation of this book under the title *The Incoherence of the Incoherence*. The writer of this book was Ibn-Rushd (Averroes in Latin) (d. 1198). He was more of an Aristotelian than a Neoplatonist, and had written commentaries on a number of the works of Aristotle. Because he lived in Spain and North Africa, his work had little influence in the centre and east of the Islamic world; but, as will be seen in the next section, it had the greatest importance for Western Europe when translated into Latin. Both Avicenna and Averroes have prominent places in world philosophy as a whole.

Averroes was the last of the philosophers in the west and centre of the Islamic world, and in the Islamic east after Avicenna there was little pure philosophy, but this may be due to reasons other than the refutation by al-Ghazali. Philosophical thinking certainly continued in the Iranian sphere, but it tended to merge into theosophy. The most important of these Iranian thinkers was Mulla Sadra (d. 1640).

4. THE INTELLECTUAL INFLUENCE OF ISLAM ON WESTERN EUROPE

Something that is not widely appreciated in the West is that Islam had a considerable influence on the intellectual life of Western Europe. This came about through the existence of an Islamic state or states in Spain from the eighth to the fifteenth centuries. The Islamic conquest of Spain and its eventual loss have already been described (Chapter 2, section 2). In Islamic Spain there was a large 'protected minority' of Christians, and these seem to have mixed more freely with the Muslims than in other Islamic provinces. The Christians were probably attracted by the higher material culture of the Muslims and wanted to share in it, while the Muslims adopted some traditional Spanish practices. The result was a partly unified common Hispano-Arabic culture. This eventually came to include all the intellectual culture of the Islamic world, which by this time had reached considerable heights, for Spain had close contacts with the centres further east.

It was formerly supposed by Western scholars that the Muslims were no more than mere transmitters of Greek science and philosophy, but it is now realized that they added considerably to what they received from the Greeks. One point was that they developed mathematics in various directions. This was admitted by a writer in the first edition of *The Legacy of Islam* (Oxford: Clarendon Press, 1931), Baron Carra de Vaux, who was no great admirer of the Arabs:

> The Arabs have really achieved great things in science; they taught the use of ciphers [Arabic numerals], although they did not invent them, and thus became the founders of the arithmetic of everyday life; they made algebra an exact science and developed it considerably and laid the foundations of analytical geometry; they were indisputably the founders of plane and spherical trigonometry which, properly speaking, did not exist among the Greeks.

In astronomy, by simplifying the mathematics and by making very careful observations they were able to produce more accurate astronomical tables. Astronomy was important for them because it enabled them to fix the direction of Mecca, which Muslims face in worship. In botany they made careful lists of plants, with special attention to those useful in pharmacology. The advances in medicine made by the Muslims are specially noteworthy. After the conquest of Iraq, they relied for a century or two on the existing Christian medical schools, but in the course of time they developed their own. Some Muslim doctors became highly skilled, for they combined clinical practice with wide theoretical knowledge. In the five centuries up to 1300 the names are known of seventy Muslim physicians who wrote medical works in Arabic. The most important was *The Canon of Medicine* of Avicenna, who has already been mentioned as a philosopher. Virtually all of this scientific material was known in Spain.

The end of Umayyad rule in Spain in 1031 led in due course to what is known as the Reconquista. An important step in this was the fall of Toledo to the Christians in 1085, because many Muslim and Jewish scholars continued to live there and could be contacted by Christian scholars from France and elsewhere. In the century after the fall of Toledo, many translations of Arabic books began to be made into Latin. The Qur'an was one such, and was followed by refutations. Western Europe certainly gained a fuller knowledge of Islam than it had previously had, despite its earlier contacts; but at the same time, it formed a negative image of Islam which has influenced European thought until the present century.

Astronomical studies in Western Europe are said to owe much to a Spanish Jew turned Christian who called himself Pedro Alfonso. He came to England in 1110 as court physician, and stimulated many scholars there and in France. More general scientific studies also developed under the influence of translations from Arabic. The effective introduction of Arabic numerals into Europe to replace the Roman numerals came about through the publication in 1202 of a book by a merchant from Pisa who had studied under a Muslim teacher in Algeria. The most important impact on Western Europe was probably that of Islamic medicine. There were already medical schools but they were distinctly backward. Contact with Islamic medicine greatly raised their standards and extended their competence. Numerous Arabic works were translated into Latin, but the predominant one was *The Canon* of Avicenna, which until about 1600 had more influence on the European medical schools than the works of Galen and Hippocrates. It was only gradually, too, that European hospitals were established and brought up to the standards set by Muslim hospitals.

In Western Europe before 1100 a little was known about Aristotelian logic, but not much else about Greek philosophy. After that date, however, Christian theologians became interested and studied the numerous translations from Arabic which were now being made. Among these were the philosophical works of Avicenna, including the exposition of his views by al-Ghazali, and nearly all those of Averroes. By the thirteenth century there was a vigorous intellectual movement which was soon to develop further what had been learned from the Muslims in science and philosophy, though not for a time in medicine. Of the philosophical works, the Aristotelian commentaries of Averroes probably had the greatest influence. One group of Christian thinkers was known as the Latin Averroists, but they aligned themselves with the more sceptical side of his philosophy, and were regarded as heretics by other Christian scholars. Much more important was the influence of the Aristotelianism of Averroes on theologians of the Dominican monastic order, and notably Thomas Aquinas (1226–74). The latter largely accepted the thought of Aristotle, though this had hitherto been regarded with suspicion by Christian scholars; and on this basis he produced a comprehensive philosophical and theological system which is still considered one of the fullest and best intellectual accounts of Christian belief.

By the fourteenth century, however, the Western European outlook was beginning to change. The poet Dante (1265–1321), in his great work *The Divine Comedy*, at one point speaks of the philosophers and mentions Avicenna and Averroes, but at the same time he has the names of a dozen Greek philosophers, and calls Aristotle 'the master of those who know'. By this time there were already one or two translations made directly from Greek, and the trickle became a flood after the conquest of Constantinople by the Ottomans in 1453, when many Greek manuscripts were brought to the West. There then developed what can only be called a revulsion of feeling from things Arabic and Islamic. Latin Christendom completely lost awareness of all that it had been given by Islamic thinkers, seeing instead everything as having come directly from the Greeks. This virtual denial of the Islamic contribution is now urgently in need of correction.

5. SUNNITE THEOLOGY AFTER AL-GHAZALI

Ash'arite theology continued to flourish for centuries after al-Ghazali, and indeed up until the present day, though latterly the theologians seem no longer to call themselves Ash'arites. The Maturidite theologians also flourished for a time, especially in the heyday of the Ottoman empire, but after that are not much heard of. An important Ash'arite theologian who lived about a century after al-Ghazali was Fakhr-ad-din ar-Razi (1149–1210). He made more use of philosophical ideas than al-Ghazali had, but in dogmatic matters was more conservative. After the sacking of Baghdad in 1258, there seems to have been a kind of cultural decline, though the reasons for this are not clear. There was, if anything, more attention given to theology, but little originality was shown. Most of the writing done seems to have consisted of commentaries and super-commentaries and glosses on these. Mention might be made of 'Adud-ad-din al-Iji (c.1281–1355), who lived mainly in Shiraz in Iran. He composed a short creed known as the *'Adudiyya* (translated in my *Islamic Creeds*) and a long theological treatise, *Al-Mawaqif*. A commentary on the latter by al-Jurjani (1340–1413) runs into four large volumes, and more than half of this is devoted to philosophical preliminaries. For the six centuries up to 1850 there is a vast amount of theological writing in manuscript, but little of it has been published and it has not been studied to any great extent.

Mention might also be made of two competent Ash'arite theologians who distinguished themselves in other fields. One is al-Baydawi (d. 1316 or earlier), who was active as a judge in Shiraz and Tabriz. He wrote a comprehensive work on Kalam but is primarily known for his commentary on the Qur'an. This summarizes, and where necessary corrects, earlier commentators, and is commonly regarded as the most authoritative of all Sunnite commentaries. The other is Ibn-Khaldun (1332–1406), who lived in various parts of North Africa, including Egypt, and as a young man wrote on theology. His fame, however, rests on his vast world history, and especially on the three-volume *Muqaddima* or *Introduction*, for in this he incorporates many original insights in the fields of sociology and the philosophy of history, in which he was a pioneer. The importance of this work has been widely recognized by European scholars. It is available in an English translation.

While in this later period Ash'arite theology gives signs of stagnation, Hanbalite theology showed great vitality. Under the 'Abbasids it had been concentrated in Baghdad, but before the invasion of Baghdad in 1258 Hanbalite groups had been formed in other cities, and after that date Damascus became the main centre. The greatest of the later Hanbalites was Ibn-Taymiyya (1263–1328), who lived mostly in Damascus but also for a few years in Cairo, as both of these places were under Mamluk rule. He was no mere academic theologian, but made public protests against what he thought was contrary to the Shari'a, such as some Sufi practices and the cult of saints. This led to spells of imprisonment and he finally died in prison. Not only did he strongly defend the Hanbalite theological position but he also made a vigorous attack on the whole tradition of Kalam. The basis of this attack was his belief that the being of God is something which the human mind cannot fully grasp, and that therefore claims to do so by the rational methods of Kalam are fatally flawed.

There were other Hanbalite theologians in the following century or two, though not of so commanding a stature. The continuing influence of Ibn-Taymiyya is thought to have led to the rise of the Wahhabite movement. The founder of this movement was Muhammad ibn 'Abd al-Wahhab (1703–92), whose home was in central Arabia but who studied in Medina and then in various centres from Cairo to Isfahan. Deeply concerned about the decadence of popular religion, he came to see that in the practical side of the thought of Ibn-Taymiyya there was guidance about how it might be reformed. He emphasized above all the need for a return to the purity of the original Islam. On his return to central Arabia, he became closely associated with the emir of a small town, who belonged to the Su'udi family, and together they achieved a measure of reform. The association of the Su'udi family with the followers of Ibn 'Abd al-Wahhab continued, with some downs as well as ups, until the twentieth century, when in 1930 the kingdom of Saudi (Su'udi) Arabia was established.

6. SHI'ITE THEOLOGY

In the first section of this chapter an account was given of the development of the Shi'ite movement and the formation of the three branches, the Zaydites, the Isma'ilites and the Imamites. In each of these groups the defence of their distinctive position required some theological thinking. That of the Zaydites was closely linked with the teaching of the Mu'tazilites, though it was not identical. Some of the Zaydite leaders were interested in theology and produced many books, but none of these seems to have had much influence outside their own sect, except perhaps among the Mu'tazilites. Some idea of the thinking of the Isma'ilites can be gained from a book entitled *A Creed of the Fatimids* by W. Ivanow (Bombay: Qayyimah Press, 1936). This is an abbreviated translation of a long credal statement composed about 1200. Although the Isma'ilites had some contacts with the main trends of Islamic thought, they developed no philosophical theology of their own.

Until 1500 the Imamites were more of a theological party than a distinct sect, living among the Sunnites and seeming to mingle freely with them. There were Imamite theologians who did not merely formulate their distinctive beliefs but also shared in the movement of thought which led to the development of Sunnite Kalam or philosophical theology. Many of these Imamite theologians were, if anything, more philosophically minded than the Sunnites. An exposition of Imamite beliefs by Ibn-Babawayh (d. 991) has been translated by Asaf A. A. Fyzee under the title *A Shi'ite Creed* (London: Oxford University Press, 1941), and there were various other Imamite theologians in the following centuries. The most important theologian of the thirteenth century was Nasir-ad-din at-Tusi (1201–74) who was deeply interested in philosophy. A short creed by one of his pupils who is usually known as 'Allama-i-Hilli (1250–1325) is reproduced in my *Islamic Creeds*, pp. 86–9, and shows the influence of philosophy on Imamite thinking.

The relation of the Imamites to the Sunnites changed completely after the establishment of the Safavid dynasty in Iran in 1501, and the declaration that Imamism was the official religion there. Imamites were now regarded as enemies by Sunnites such as the Ottoman sultans; and they tended to be concentrated in Iran, though a few groups maintained an existence in Syria and elsewhere. Under the Safavids, theological discussions continued, but fresh questions arose. In the seventeenth century a split occurred between groups known as the Akhbarites and the Usulites. The former held that legal opinions should be based on *akhbar* – that is, reports of something said by Muhammad or by one of their twelve imams – while the latter defended the right of qualified jurists to derive particular rules from general principles (*usul*) by some form of reasoning.

Apart from this special problem, there were thinkers working out theological and philosophical elaborations of Imamite doctrine, and also bringing in mystical elements. The most distinguished of these was Mulla Sadra (d. 1640), but some Western students of his works have thought that he was moving from philosophy into what was rather theosophy, and the high claims for his importance made by Iranian scholars have not been generally accepted in the West. After the seventeenth century no outstanding work was produced by an Imamite thinker, but there are now signs of a renewal of intellectual activity.

7. SUFISM

In Muhammad himself there was a deep mystical element, although not much of this found expression in the external forms of the Islamic religion. After his death, however, some devout and pious Muslims began to spend more time in meditation on religious themes and to engage in ascetic practices. One such was al-Hasan al-Basri (643–728), who was also at the centre of the early theological discussions in Basra. Some of these early ascetics dressed in wool (*suf*), and the later mystics came to be known as Sufis and their practice as Sufism (*tasawwuf*), even where the mystical side predominated over the ascetic.

One of the pioneers in the mystical quest was a woman, Rabi'a al-Adawiyya (d. 801). While some of the ascetics had been chiefly moved by fear of God and the Last Judgement, she sought a deeper knowledge of God and became more aware of his love for human beings, and was herself taken up into a deep experience of love for him. In the following century this trend continued and developed, and the profound experiences which some persons underwent led them to claim that they had achieved a unity with God. This naturally enraged the theologians, for they regarded God and humanity as essentially different from one another. Among these people was al-Hallaj (d. 922), who is reported to have said, 'I am he whom I love and he whom I love is I' and 'I am the Truth' (where Truth is understood as a name of God). He went about proclaiming his faith, and was finally arrested by the authorities and cruelly executed. An exhaustive study of al-Hallaj was made by the French scholar Louis Massignon (d. 1962), whose faith in God after a period of scepticism had been restored by contacts with believing Muslims. His great work *The Passion of al-Hallaj, Mystic and Martyr* was published in four volumes in an English translation by Herbert Mason.

In the following two centuries various persons tried to combine Sufi practice with an acceptance of the five pillars and standard Islamic dogma. In this field the most important advance was made by al-Ghazali, who has already been spoken of as a theologian. In his great book *The Revival of the Religious Sciences*, he shows among other things how a Sufi way of life can be combined with observance of the five daily acts of worship and other basic duties of a Muslim. A simplified version of this is contained in a small book, *The Beginning of Guidance* (of which a translation forms the second half of my *Faith and Practice of al-Ghazâlî*). The writings and example of al-Ghazali seem to have led to a greater tolerance for Sufism among theologians, and it began to spread more widely. This also raised the level of popular religion in many parts of the Islamic world, and enabled Islam to enter more deeply into the lives of populations which had hitherto been little more than nominally Muslim.

About a century after al-Ghazali there was another out-standing thinker whose influence was in the opposite direction. This was Muhyi-d-din ibn-al-'Arabi (1165–1240), originally from Spain, who has left voluminous writings. In these he took various speculative Sufi ideas and elaborated them into a systematic mystical theology, not altogether self-coherent. This, he claimed, was in line with standard Islamic doctrine, but in fact it verged on pantheism. Many Sufis in the eastern Islamic world were attracted by his system and partly followed it, but the main Sufi orders held aloof.

The twelfth century saw the beginnings of the Sufi orders. For at least a century previously, groups of Sufis had been joining together for special acts of worship and other purposes. Al-Ghazali himself had gathered a band of disciples round him. Very popular was the *dhikr* (literally 'mention'), in which members of the group recited together passages of the Qur'an or the names of God or other religious texts. In the twelfth century such groups became more formally organized, often with initiation ceremonies. Groups tended to form round leaders with exceptional religious gifts. Although the Qur'an discouraged celibacy and encouraged marriage, and the earlier Sufis had normally been married, by the twelfth century those who came into the orders often thought of themselves as 'poor men' or 'mendicants' (*faqir, darwish*) and were unmarried. Such men also began to live together in what was called a *ribat*. This word seems originally to have meant a frontier fortress, but as used by the Sufi orders it was virtually a monastery. Somewhat exceptionally, the Safawiyya order developed into the military basis for the establishment of the Safavid dynasty in Iran in 1501; and in the Ottoman empire the corps of Janissaries was closely connected with the Bektashiyya order.

One of the earliest organized orders was the Qadiriyya (not to be confused with the heretical sect of the Qadariyya or Qadarites). This order grew up round 'Abd-al-Qadir al-Jilani (1077–1166), who was a Hanbalite jurist but had had deep mystical experiences. A *ribat* was built for him outside Baghdad, and to this disciples flocked. The order soon spread to other parts of western Asia and to Egypt, and developed many suborders. Another important order was the Shadhiliyya, founded by ash-Shadhili (d. 1258) in Alexandria, which later spread into North Africa and Arabia. Very popular among the Ottoman Turks was the Bektashi order, which departed at many points from standard Islam. The Mevlevi order or Mawlawiyya, founded by Jalal-ad-din ar-Rumi (d. 1273) at Konya, never spread widely, but because its members used music and dancing in their *dhikr*, they became known as the 'whirling dervishes'. In the light of the Indian mystical tradition, it is not surprising to find many Sufi orders in India, both the universal ones such as the Qadiriyya and the Naqshbandiyya, and also many others peculiar to the subcontinent.

As an order became more fully organized and acquired a distinctive character, it tended to attract many supporters or adherents who did not become full members of the order but participated in its life in various ways. A distinction has sometimes been drawn between those orders whose members and adherents were drawn entirely from town-dwellers and those which attracted country people from the villages. With the increase in numbers, many non-Islamic practices tended to creep in, especially in the country orders, where local traditions were still alive. In India Hindu mystical tradition affected many of the orders, and some Indian theologians tried to correct this tendency by reformulating standard theology in a way that was more favourable to a moderate Sufism. The best known of these is Shah Wali-Allah of Delhi (1702–62).

It is difficult to give a balanced picture of Sufism. On the one hand, there are some wonderful writings whose mystical depths have attracted many Westerners, but on the other, the Sufi orders have had both successes and failures. In their earlier days, they certainly brought about a widespread growth of religion among the ordinary people, who had been quite unable to follow the mental gymnastics of the theologians as they became more and more absorbed in academic niceties. As time went on, however, some of the orders drifted away from the mainstream of Islam in ways which led to an impoverishment of their religious content. There was a certain amount of charlatanism, and we hear of the full members of an order leading a lazy and luxurious life, using the contributions of poor villagers who supported them. It is little wonder, then, that some educated Muslims are strongly opposed to the Sufi orders for other than purely theological reasons. The subject is so vast, however, that it is impossible to have an overall view of the condition of Sufism and the Sufi orders at the present time.

6 THE CHALLENGE OF THE MODERN WORLD

It remains to say something about the great changes which have taken place in the world in the present century, especially the last half-century, and about how these affect Islam and Muslim–Christian relations. To understand these changes, however, we must go further back.

1. THE ADVANCE OF EUROPE AND THE WEST

Until about 1700 the Ottoman empire and the Western European countries were roughly equal in military power. Even before then, however, the Europeans had been developing in ways which the Muslims were unable to follow. From the Muslims the Western Europeans had learned methods of improving sailing ships, and this ultimately enabled them to produce ships capable of crossing the Atlantic and other oceans. This led to the discovery of America by Columbus in 1492, but more important for European–Muslim relations was the discovery by Vasco da Gama in 1498 of the route round the Cape of Good Hope to the East Indies. This led to a great growth in trade by this route – trade that was entirely in the hands of the Europeans. For reasons that are not clear, the Muslims of India and Indonesia did not send their ships in the opposite direction, despite their long tradition of seafaring.

The Europeans first made treaties with local rulers for the establishment of depots and trading stations. Sometimes, however, it became necessary to send soldiers to protect these from raiders. As trade increased and spread over a wider area, the Europeans began to exercise a degree of control over some regions; and this was gradually extended until it took the form of colonies. The countries engaging in this trade were Portugal, the Netherlands, France and Britain; but the Portuguese became more interested in trade with South America, and the French colonies in India were seized by the British during the Napoleonic wars. European settlements in Africa also developed into colonies.

While this was happening, Europe was also developing in other ways. It became militarily stronger than the Ottomans as a result of improvements in guns and other weapons. After this there were more and more inventions, leading to the Industrial Revolution. In the early nineteenth century new factories were springing up to manufacture new types of goods. It was discovered how to use steam power to drive stationary machines and then to enable a locomotive to pull a train of wagons or carriages. Later came discoveries about how to use electricity for many purposes, and how to use petroleum and other fuel oils to drive cars and aeroplanes. All the discoveries and inventions led to greatly increased trade between Europe (now joined by North America to form 'the West') and the rest of the world.

Muslim reactions to all these developments are complex. The wealthier Muslims in all countries wanted a share of the comforts and luxuries which the West now provided, while Muslim rulers wanted military hardware to strengthen their own positions at home and sometimes also to dominate their neighbours. As already mentioned, the rulers of Egypt had borrowed so much money from Europe in order to acquire all the goods they wanted that in 1882 a British force was sent to Egypt to ensure the repayment of the debts and the interest.

At the intellectual level, however, the position was somewhat different. The traditionalist religious scholars or intellectuals of the Ottoman empire continued to accept the view that Muhammad was the last of the prophets and that the Qur'an contained God's final and perfect message for the human race. Because of this belief, they took for granted that they had nothing to learn from any other philosophical or religious system, and so they made no attempt to understand the scientific thinking that was at the basis of the European inventions and was part of a wider Western intellectual outlook. They did not even think it worth while studying this outlook in order to refute its faults. When young Ottoman subjects came to Western Europe as diplomats or merchants, they had no preparation for dealing with the intellectual world into which they would be plunged.

In India this attitude also existed. As the British extended their rule in India, they established an education system of a European type in order to train Indians for posts in the administration. The Hindus seized this opportunity gladly, but many Muslims were suspicious of Western education and did not send their sons to the British schools. The result was that there were proportionately far more Hindus than Muslims in all grades of the administration; and this was one of the reasons for the Indian Mutiny of 1857, in which most of the mutineers were Muslim. The failure of the mutiny and the ensuing abolition of the Mogul empire led to dejection among many Muslims. In this situation an important lead in a new direction was given by Sir Sayyid Ahmad Khan (1817–98). So that Muslims could play their part in the India of the future, he encouraged them to allow their children to have a Western-type education, assuring them that there was nothing in it contrary to Islamic faith. Many Muslims accepted his views and sent their children to the schools. In 1875, in furtherance of his aims, he founded what he called the Muhammadan Anglo-Oriental College, which later became the University of Aligarh. He himself was bitterly attacked by 'ulama' and other conservatives and denounced as a heretic. The Mufti of Medina even issued a fatwa condemning him to death. Another modernist, Ameer Ali (1849–1928), wrote a book, called in later editions *The Spirit of Islam*, in which he tried to show that the Islamic religion embodied all the values admired by Westerners.

Despite the opposition of traditionalist 'ulama' throughout the Islamic world, many responsible Muslims realized the importance of a Western-type education. At the beginning of the nineteenth century in Egypt Muhammad 'Ali saw that he could not have a modern army on the European model (for which he was planning) unless his officers had some education of a European type; and for this purpose he brought teachers from Europe to Egypt. From this beginning the Western type of education gradually spread, until by the beginning of the twentieth century Egypt had a complete system extending from primary schools to a university. This existed alongside the traditional Islamic form of education, which went from local Qur'an schools to the ancient university of al-Azhar. By the later 1920s there was something similar in nearly all Islamic countries. While traditional Islamic education continued to exist, an ever-growing proportion of the population was sending their children to the Western-type schools.

After the First World War the former Ottoman provinces of Syria and Lebanon were placed under French mandate and Palestine, Transjordan and Iraq under British mandate. Some thought this was a new name for 'colony', but colonialism was really on its way out. Iraq became independent in 1932, and the others during or immediately after the Second World War, except that Palestine was divided between Israel and the kingdom of

Jordan. Egypt had become partly independent as early as 1922, and fully independent later. In 1947 British India became the independent states of Pakistan and India. At later dates the North African states also became independent.

All the new independent states entered the United Nations. Colonialism was thus technically dead (with some minor exceptions), but some Muslim countries felt that it had been replaced by an economic colonialism; in other words, they were still economically dependent on the West. This point, however, brings us to the theme of the next section.

2. GLOBALIZATION

As we consider the place of Islam and other religions in the world of today, it is necessary to realize that the world in which we live is different in important ways from the world in all previous ages. The world has become a 'global village' in a way it never was before. This has come about as a result of the inventions made by the West in the last two centuries. The steam train and steamship, the automobile and the aeroplane have greatly speeded up the transport of persons and goods. Telephones and radios have speeded up the communication of ideas and commands, while television and improvements in newspaper production mean that what is regarded as news reaches ordinary people in every part of the world almost immediately.

The new inventions and the corresponding technological and industrial developments have had many important results. One is the unification of the world, or globalization. This is seen in the establishment of the United Nations. This body is criticized in various ways, but at least it provides a forum in which representatives of nearly all the inhabitants of the world can express their views. Because of the ease and rapidity of travel, statesmen and women are regularly meeting their counterparts from the remotest parts of the world. There are also changes in the structures of national communities. Greater conurbations of people have come into existence because people and goods can move about so easily, but this creates problems when masses of country people flock into the growing cities in hopes of a higher standard of living. Among the new conurbations in the Islamic world one might reckon Cairo and Karachi.

Along with the political and economic unification of the world, there goes a measure of intellectual unification. What may be called the Western intellectual outlook is now omnipresent. It is not fully accepted by everyone, of course, but the more educated people in every country are exposed to it to a great extent, because it is implicit in both the Western form of education and the products of television and other media. The Western intellectual outlook has grown out of the European Enlightenment of the eighteenth century. That movement exalted the place of human reason and was very critical of Christianity and other religions, but its successors nowadays are mostly neutral towards religion rather than hostile. The general outlook, however, has many aspects which create difficulties for religious believers. It accepts the assured results of all the sciences, including the belief that humanity has evolved from lower forms of life. It believes that the world and human society do not stand still, but are constantly changing and developing (although it is not so sure now as it was a century ago that the changes are all improvements and that the world is progressing). It attaches much importance to history, but also insists that historical statements must be carefully checked. It has evolved the discipline of literary criticism, and applied it not only to Biblical texts but also to Latin and Greek texts and to historical documents.

Muslims have been affected by all these forms of globalization or world-unification. Politically, the independent Islamic countries have become members of the United Nations, even though some of them feel that it is little more than a tool of American and Western interests. In the economic field they have wanted to share in all the goods the West has to offer, not least in its armaments, and this has been particularly easy for those which have acquired great oil wealth. Some Islamic countries have also tried to develop industrial production on Western lines, though none has been nearly so successful as the Japanese. Many Islamic countries have even formed football teams to take part in world competitions. When one begins to look more widely, however, especially at the intellectual position, the situation becomes more complex.

Especially since about 1970 there has been taking place a resurgence of the Islamic religion. This is by no means a unitary movement, but has many different manifestations. It is in part a response to globalization, and, though there have been similar phenomena in other religions, it has distinctive Islamic features. The medieval idea of a firm distinction between the sphere of Islam and the sphere of war (*dar al-Islam, dar al-harb*) still has some influence. This idea developed at a time when Islam was expanding and Muslims hoped that their religion would soon be accepted by the whole world as the final religion. Regions which were not yet under Muslim control were regarded as hostile, and thus places where war was possible and perhaps necessary. There is probably much less thought now about the sphere of war, but there is still some acceptance of the idea of the sphere of Islam as a part of the world which is different from the rest of it.

This belief in the difference of Islam from the rest of the world shows itself in various ways. There are attempts to create enclaves that are purely Muslim. Even Saudi Arabia, although it welcomes non-Muslims to help with various projects, forbids public forms of non-Muslim worship. While male statesmen in most non-European countries adopt European dress, Arab statesmen retain Arab dress. Yasser Arafat, the representative of the Palestinians, retains at least his *keffiyeh* (head-dress). In France there have been troubles because Muslim traditionalists wanted their girls to wear headscarves. Where existing legal systems have incorporated Western ideas, there have been attempts to replace these by a return to the original form of Islam. It is not clearly recognized that this desire to be purely Islamic is not compatible with the desire to share in the material aspects of the life of the rest of the world, and is in danger of relegating the Muslims to a ghetto.

Much of the resurgence is labelled by the Western media as 'Islamic fundamentalism', but this is an inappropriate term. 'Fundamentalism' applies primarily to certain forms of Protestant Christianity. A somewhat similar trend in Roman Catholicism is called in French *intégrisme*. Neither of these terms, however, is properly applied to Islamic movements. It would be better to speak of traditionalism. This comprises many different groups, some hoping that the return to an earlier Islam can be brought about by peaceful methods, but others with militant political programmes; and there are still other groups for which neither term is appropriate.

At the opposite extreme from the traditionalists are those who may be called liberals. They are convinced that Muslims will not be able to share in the life of the world unless they come to terms with the Western intellectual outlook. They are therefore trying to restate basic Islamic beliefs in ways that are compatible with this position, or at least not obviously incompatible. This, of course, leaves them open to severe criticism from the traditionalists, as happened in the case of Sir Sayyid Ahmad Khan in India. In Egypt a beginning was made by the theologian Muhammad 'Abduh (1849–1905), who became head of the traditional university of al-Azhar and Grand Mufti of Egypt. He set about reforming teaching at al-Azhar and advocated legal reforms. His ideas are expressed in a book, *Risalat at-tawhid* (*The Theology of Unity*), but this shows that he is still nearer to the traditionalists than to later liberals. Certain later Muslim thinkers have become much more adventurous. Among those who are still alive might be mentioned Mohammed Arkoun, an Algerian who is a professor in Paris, Mahmoud Ayoub, a Lebanese who is a professor in the United States, and Akbar Ahmed, a Pakistani who is presently a visiting professor in Cambridge.

3. THE PROBLEMS FACING ISLAM TODAY

After this very brief outline of how Muslims have been trying to deal with globalization, a word may be said about the problems still facing Islam, as these are seen by an outsider. Because the Western intellectual outlook now dominates the world through the various media, it is essential that Muslims should learn to live with it, while retaining their basic beliefs. Thus the idea of development has a central place in the Western outlook, whereas the pre-Arabian idea, taken over by Muslims in general, was that the world is unchanging. It may be true that the forms of nomadic life in Arabia changed little from the time of Muhammad to the beginning of the present century, but it is also clear that there have been great changes in the world in the course of globalization. In so far as social structures have changed and we now have great conurbations in which vast numbers of people are herded together, it is unreasonable to suppose that a return to the Islam of Muhammad and the rightly guided caliphs is literally possible. The basic legal ideas of Islam are sound, but they need to be adapted to the changed circumstances of today.

An attitude to historical events features largely in the Western outlook, and this leads to questions about the truth of some traditionalist conceptions of the history of Islam. Was the period of the rightly guided caliphs really an ideal period? After all, three of them were assassinated. Were the Umayyads so un-Islamic as is commonly supposed? One could continue asking such questions, but the central point would seem to be that, even when traditional ideas about the history of one's religion are inaccurate or even downright mistaken, this does not affect the basic doctrinal beliefs. One can radically revise inherited ideas about the history of Islam and still be a good Muslim.

The discipline of literary criticism is associated with the historical outlook. As applied to the Bible, it has caused Christians to make an extensive revision of their ideas about how the Bible reached its present form. Since the Qur'an, however, was revealed within a quarter of a century, and finally collected shortly afterwards, there are no similar problems connected with it. All that literary criticism might deal with is the dating of the various passages and the way in which passages from different dates were brought together to form suras.

The scientific and philosophical aspects of the Western outlook raise problems for all religions. This is a field in which Muslim scholars still have much work to do, though some have already made useful contributions. For over a century, Christian scholars have been trying to reach an understanding of the being and activity of God which does not contradict the assured results of science, even if it contradicts some of the other ideas thought to be scientific; and in this matter some important advances have been made. Muslims might have something to learn from Christian thinkers. One of the problems to be tackled is the contradiction between the statement that God created the world in six days and the scientific assertion that there has been a long process of evolution of plant and animal life. Some Muslims have argued that scientists are not agreed about evolution and that therefore it need not be accepted; but this is mistaken. What scientists disagree about is the nature of the factors causing the evolutionary process; but no scientist denies that there has been a long evolutionary process stretching over millions of years. The religious believer who wants to accept the ideas both of creation and of evolution needs to enter into a profound consideration of the nature of religious truth, and of the various ways in which this truth may be expressed, such as literal and metaphorical, pictorial and poetic.

Apart from coming to terms with the Western intellectual outlook, Muslims also need to do more thinking about the place of Islam in the world. At the political level, Islamic countries have certainly been able to play a part in the United Nations. At the level of everyday life, they are setting up industries on a Western model and entering world football competitions. So far, however, they have not done much thinking about the relation of Islam to other religions, despite the fact that in the present age the adherents of different religions are mingling with one another to a much greater extent than in any previous age. The basic question is whether Islam is different from all other religious and philosophical systems, so that the idea of a distinctive sphere of Islam still makes sense, or simply one religion among many, even if it is in some ways superior to the others. Muslims of a liberal turn of mind seem to accept in practice that there are other religions which are more or less on a level with Islam, but many traditionalists appear still to think that Islam has a wholly unique position in the religious field.

For Islam to take its proper place in a multireligious world, it is important that Muslims should admit that there is at least a large measure of truth in other religions. An increasing activity in today's world is dialogue between different religions, both at a formal and official level and more informally; and this is something in which many Muslims are already involved. There are other areas too in which co-operation between the religions might lead to improvements in world affairs. Most religions would want to uphold the importance of the family in a world in which family breakdown is becoming a problem. It is also agreed that a reform of the United Nations is required in order to make the organization both more impartial and more effective; and here a committee composed of representatives of different religions could make an important contribution.

APPENDIX

The Creed of al-Ash'ari

The dogmatic position finally adopted by al-Ash'ari is expressed in a creed which he included in his book on the Islamic sects and which is translated in my *Islamic Creed* (pp. 41–7). It is reproduced here as an example of a Sunnite creed. The word 'amodally' in articles 7 and 8 renders an Arabic phrase, literally 'without how', which was used by the Hanbalites to insist that the anthropomorphic terms applied to God were to be accepted without asking whether they were literal or metaphorical. The term 'acting-power' is used for the Arabic *istita'a* in article 15, because it was held that the power to act which God creates in a person at the moment of acting was different from the power (*qudra*) exercised by God himself.

1. The sum of what is held by those following the Hadiths and the Sunna is the confession of God, his angels, his books, his messengers, what has come [as revelation] from God, and what trustworthy [persons] have related from the Messenger of God.
2. God is one deity, unique, eternal; there is no deity except him; he has not taken to himself consort or child.
3. Muhammad is his servant and messenger.
4. Paradise is a reality and Hell is a reality.
5. The Hour is undoubtedly coming, and God will raise up those in the tombs.

6. God is on his throne; as he said: 'The Merciful on the throne is seated' (20.5).

7. God has two hands [to be understood] amodally; as he said: '[What] I created with my two hands' (38.75), and: 'Nay, his two hands are spread out [in bounty]' (5.64).

8. God has two eyes [to be understood] amodally; as he said: 'which sailed before our eyes' (54.14).

9. God has a face; as he said: 'The face of your Lord endures, full of majesty and honour' (55.27).

10. The names of God are not said to be other than God, as the Mu'tazilites and the Kharijites affirmed.

11. They assert that God possesses knowledge; as he said: 'He sent it down with his knowledge' (4.166), and: 'No female conceives and brings to birth [a child] without his knowledge' (35.11).

12. They affirm hearing and sight of God, and do not deny that as do the Mu'tazilites.

13. They affirm that God has power; as he said: 'Did they not see that God who created them was mightier than they in power?' (41.15).

14. They hold that on earth there is neither good nor evil except what God wills, and that things come to be by the will of God; as he said: 'But you will not will [anything] unless God wills [it]' (81.29); and, as the Muslims say: 'What God wills comes to be, and what he does not will does not come to be.'

15. They hold that [a person] has no acting-power to do anything before he [actually] does it, and that he is not able to escape God's knowledge or to do a thing which God knows he will not do.

16. They assert that there is no creator except God, that the evil actions of human beings are created by God and that the

[good] works of human beings are created by God, and that human beings are not able to create anything.

17. They assert that God helps [or succours] the believers in obeying him and abandons the unbelievers. He shows favour to the believers, has compassion on them, makes them sound [persons] and guides them; but he does not show favour to the unbelievers or make them sound or guide them. If he made [the latter] sound, they would be sound [indeed], and if he guided them, they would be guided [aright]. God does have power to make the unbelievers sound and to show favour to them so that they become believers; but he willed not to make the unbelievers sound and to show favour to them so that they became believers; [on the contrary] he willed that they should be unbelievers, as he knew [they would be], and he abandoned them, sent them astray and put a seal on their hearts.

18. [They assert] that good and evil are by God's decree and pre-determination; and they believe in God's decree and predetermination [both] of the good and the evil, of the sweet and the bitter.

19. They believe that they do not control [things] beneficial or harmful for themselves, except what God wills, as he has said.

20. They commit their affair to God and affirm [their] need of him at all times and [their] want of him in all circumstances.

21. They hold that the Qur'an is the speech of God and uncreated. [In respect of] the discussion about suspending judgement [as to whether the Qur'an is created or not] or [about holding that our] utterance [of the Qur'an is created], they consider that he who holds the utterance [to be created] or who suspends judgement [on uncreatedness] is an innovator. [Our] utterance of the Qur'an is not said to be created, nor is it said to be uncreated.

22. They hold that God will be seen by the eyes on the day of resurrection, as the moon is seen on the night when it is full. The believers will see him, but the unbelievers will not see him, for they will be veiled from God. God has said: 'Nay, but on that day from their Lord they will be veiled' (83.15). [They hold] that Moses asked God for the vision [of him] in this life, and that God appeared to the mountain and levelled it, thus informing [Moses] that he would not see him in this life but would see him in the life to come (7.143).

23. They do not declare any of the people of the qibla to be an unbeliever because of a sin which he commits, such as adultery, theft and similar great sins.

24. Faith, according to them, is faith in God, his angels, his books, his messengers, and in the predetermination [by God] of [both] the good and the evil, the sweet and the bitter; and [faith] that what missed them could not have hit them, and that what hit them could not have missed them. Islam is bearing witness that there is no deity except God and that Muhammad is the Messenger of God, in accordance with what has come in the Hadiths. Islam in their view is other than faith.

25. They assert that God is the changer of hearts.

26. They assert the intercession of the Messenger of God, and that it is on behalf of great sinners of his community.

27. [They assert] that the punishment of the tomb [is a reality], that the Basin is a reality, that the Bridge is a reality, that resurrection after death is a reality, that God's reckoning with human beings is a reality, and that the standing before God is a reality.

28. They assert that faith is speech and action [or works], and that it increases and decreases; they do not state that it is [either] created or uncreated.

29. They hold that the Names of God are God.

30. They do not bear witness of Hell [being certain] for any great sinner, nor do they judge that Paradise [is certain] for any monotheist, until it comes about that God has placed them where he willed. They say that the affair of these [persons] belongs to God; if he wills, he punishes them, and if he wills, he forgives them.

31. They believe that [by the intercession of the Messenger of God] God will bring out a group of the monotheists from Hell, according to what has been related from the Messenger of God.

32. They disapprove of disputation and quarrelling about religion, of contention over predestination, and of argument over that in their religion about which the disputatious argue and disagree; [that is] because of their [own] acceptance of soundly based [report] and of what has come in the accounts related by trustworthy [persons], just [person] from just [person], until [the chain of transmission] ends with the Messenger of God. They do not say 'How?' or 'Why?', because that is innovation.

33. They hold that God did not command evil, but forbade it and commanded good; and that he did not approve of evil even though he willed it.

34. They recognize the virtue of the predecessors whom God chose for the companionship of his Prophet; and they keep [speaking about] their merits, and they refrain from [speaking about] what was disputed between them, [both] the lesser and the greater of them.

35. They set in the foremost [place] Abu-Bakr, then 'Umar, then 'Uthman, then 'Ali, and they assert that these were the rightly and truly guided caliphs, the most excellent of all the people after the Prophet.

36. They count true Hadiths which have come from the Messenger of God [stating] that God descends to the lowest heaven and says: 'Is there anyone who asks forgiveness?'
37. They hold closely to the book and the Sunna; as God said: 'If you dispute about anything, refer it to God and the Messenger' (4.59). They think it proper to follow the ancient imams of the religion, and not to introduce [as an innovation] into their religion what God has not permitted.
38. They assert that God will come on the day of resurrection; as he said: 'And your Lord will come and the angels, rank on rank' (89.22).
39. [They assert] that God draws near to his creation as he wills; as he said: 'For we [God] are nearer to him than his neck-vein' (50.16).
40. They think it proper to [worship] behind every imam, upright and sinful, on feast-days, Fridays and assemblies.
41. They affirm the moistening of the sandals as a Sunna, and think it proper [both] at home and on a journey.
42. They affirm the duty of Jihad against the polytheists from the time of God's sending of his Prophet until the last band which fights the Dajjal [a kind of Antichrist] and after that.
43. They think it proper to pray for the welfare of the imams of the Muslims, not to rebel against them with the sword, and not to fight in civil strife.
44. They count true the appearance of the Dajjal, and the killing of him by 'Isa ibn-Maryam [Jesus].
45. They believe in Munkar and Nakir [two superhuman beings who interrogate the dead in the tombs], in the ascension of Muhammad to Heaven, and in visions during sleep.
46. They believe that prayer for the Muslim dead and alms [given] on their behalf after their death reach them.

47. They think it proper to pray over all who die of the people of the qibla, both the upright and the sinners, and to accept bequests from them.

48. They assert that Paradise and Hell are [already] created.

49. They assert that he who dies dies at his appointed term, and that likewise he who is killed is killed at his appointed term.

50. [They assert] that sustaining [foods] are from God; he gives them, whether lawful or unlawful, as sustenance to human beings.

51. Satan whispers to people, makes them doubt, and renders them mad.

52. It is possible for God to mask out the upright by signs which appear for them.

53. The Sunna is not abrogated by the Qur'an.

54. The treatment of children [who die] is for God [to decide]; if he wills, he punishes them, and if he wills, he does to them what he proposes.

55. God knows what human beings will do, and has written that that will be; [all] affairs are in the hand of God.

56. They think it proper to endure patiently God's judgement, to hold fast to what God has commanded, to refrain from what God has forbidden, to be sincere in [one's] works, and to give good counsel to the Muslims.

57. They practise the worship of God along with the worshippers, the giving of good counsel to the community of the Muslims, the avoidance of great sins, adultery, speaking falsely, showing factional spirit, boasting, acting insolently, disparaging people and being unduly proud.

58. They think it proper to shun all those who summon to innovation, to be diligent in reciting the Qur'an, in writing the reports [such as Hadiths], and in reflecting on jurisprudence,

while [at the same time] being humble, submissive, and of good moral character, being generous in well-doing, refraining from [causing] injury, abstaining from backbiting, slander and calumny, and being temperate in food and drink.

This is the sum of what they command and observe and think proper. [For our part] all we have mentioned of what they hold we [also] hold and formally adopt. We have no succour except God. He is our sufficiency and the best of Guardians. To him do we call for help, in him do we trust, and to him is the [final] return.

SELECT BIBLIOGRAPHY

Note that there are later editions of a number of the works listed.

General Works

Calverley, Edwin E., 1925, *Worship in Islam*, Madras, Christian Literature Society for India.

Endress, Gerhard, 1988, *An Introduction to Islam*, trans. Carole Hillenbrand, Edinburgh: Edinburgh University Press.

Esposito, John L., 1988, *Islam: The Straight Path*, New York: Oxford University Press.

Gibb, H. A. R., 1975, *Islam: A Historical Survey*, London: Oxford University Press.

Holm, J. and Bowker, J. (eds.), 1994, *Themes in Religious Studies*, London: Pinter Publishers.

Lewis, Bernard (ed.), 1974, *Islam from the Prophet Muhammad to the Capture of Constantinople*, 2 vols., New York: Harper & Row.

Schacht, Joseph and Bosworth, C. E. (eds.), 1974, *The Legacy of Islam*, 2nd edn., Oxford: Clarendon Press.

The Career of Muhammad

Watt, William M., 1953, *Muhammad at Mecca*, Oxford: Clarendon Press.

—— 1956, *Muhammad at Medina*, Oxford, Clarendon Press.

—— 1961, *Muhammad, Prophet and Statesman*, London: Oxford University Press.

The Qur'an

There are many translations of varying merit; the following are among the most important.

Arberry, Arthur J., 1955, *The Koran Interpreted*, London: Allen & Unwin.

Cragg, Kenneth, 1995, *The Event of the Qur'án: Islam in Its Scripture*, Oxford: Oneworld.

Pickthall, Marmaduke, 1930, *The Meaning of the Glorious Koran*, London: Knopf (later Allen & Unwin).

Sale, George, 1734, *The Koran, Commonly Called the Alkoran of Mohammed*, (still being reprinted as it closely follows the standard commentary of al-Baydawi).

Watt, William M., 1994, *Companion to the Qur'án*, Oxford: Oneworld.

Watt, William M. and Bell, Richard, 1970, *Introduction to the Qur'an*, Edinburgh: Edinburgh University Press.

Islamic Law

Coulson, Noel J., 1964, *A History of Islamic Law*, Edinburgh: Edinburgh University Press.

Schacht, Joseph, 1964, *An Introduction to Islamic Law*, Oxford: Clarendon Press.

Islamic Theology

Massignon, Louis, 1982, *The Passion of al-Hallaj, Mystic and Martyr*, trans. Herbert Mason, Princeton, NJ: Princeton University Press.

Watt, William M., 1972, *The Influence of Islam on Medieval Europe*, Edinburgh: Edinburgh University Press.

—— 1985, *Islamic Philosophy and Theology*, enlarged edn., Edinburgh: Edinburgh University Press.

—— 1994, *Islamic Creeds: A Selection*, Edinburgh: Edinburgh University Press.

—— 1994, *The Faith and Practice of Al-Ghazálí*, Oxford: Oneworld.

Mysticism

Schimmel, Annemarie, 1975, *Mystical Dimensions of Islam*, Chapel Hill, NC: University of North Carolina Press.

Smith, Margaret, 1995, *Rabi'a: The Life and Work of Rabi'a and Other Women Mystics of Islam*, Oxford: Oneworld.

The Modern Period

Ahmed, Akbar, 1992, *Postmodernism and Islam: Predicament and Promise*, London: Routledge.

Bowker, J., 1995, *Voices of Islam*, Oxford: Oneworld.

Cragg, Kenneth, 1965, *Counsels in Contemporary Islam*, Edinburgh: Edinburgh University Press.

Rahman, Fazlur, 1982, *Islam and Modernity: The Transformation of an Intellectual Tradition*, Chicago: University of Chicago Press.

INDEX